Richard Harding Davis'
War in Cuba &
Spanish-American War

Richard Harding Davis

Richard Harding Davis' War in Cuba & Spanish-American War

The Articles, Letters and Experiences of One of America's Finest War Correspondents

ILLUSTRATED

Richard Harding Davis

LEONAUR

Richard Harding Davis' War in Cuba & Spanish-American War
The Articles, Letters and Experiences of One of America's Finest War Correspondents
by Richard Harding Davis

ILLUSTRATED

FIRST EDITION

First published under the titles
Cuba in Wartime
and
Adventures and Letters of Richard Harding Davis (Extract)

Leonaur is an imprint of Oakpast Ltd
Copyright in this form © 2021 Oakpast Ltd

ISBN: 978-1-78282-986-7 (hardcover)
ISBN: 978-1-78282-987-4 (softcover)

http://www.leonaur.com

Publisher's Notes

Contents

Author's Note

After my return from Cuba many people asked me questions concerning the situation there, and I noticed that they generally asked the same questions. This book has been published with the idea of answering those questions as fully as is possible for me to do after a journey through the island during which I travelled in four of the six provinces, visiting towns, seaports, plantations and military camps, and stopping for several days in all of the chief cities of Cuba, with the exception of Santiago and Pinar del Rio.

Part of this book was published originally in the form of letters from Cuba to the *New York Journal* and in the newspapers of a syndicate arranged by the *Journal*; the remainder, which was suggested by the questions asked on my return, was written in this country, and appears here for the first time.

Richard Harding Davis.

Cuba In War Time

When the revolution broke out in Cuba two years ago, (1895), the Spaniards at once began to build tiny forts, and continued to add to these and improve those already built, until now the whole island, which is eight hundred miles long and averages eighty miles in width, is studded as thickly with these little forts as is the sole of a brogan with iron nails. It is necessary to keep the fact of the existence of these forts in mind in order to understand the situation in Cuba at the present time, as they illustrate the Spanish plan of campaign, and explain why the war has dragged on for so long, and why it may continue indefinitely.

The last revolution was organised by the aristocrats; the present one is a revolution of the *puebleo*, and, while the principal Cuban families are again among the leaders, with them now are the representatives of the "plain people," and the cause is now a common cause in working for the success of which all classes of Cubans are desperately in earnest.

The outbreak of this revolution was hastened by an offer from Spain to make certain reforms in the internal government of the island. The old revolutionary leaders, fearing that the promise of these reforms might satisfy the Cubans, and that they would cease to hope for complete independence, started the revolt, and asked all loyal Cubans not to accept the so-called reforms when, by fighting, they might obtain their freedom. Another cause which precipitated the revolution was the financial depression which existed all over the island in 1894, and the closing of the sugar mills in consequence.

Owing to the lack of money with which to pay the labourers, the grinding of the sugarcane ceased, and the men were turned off by the hundreds, and, for want of something better to do, joined the insurgents. Some planters believe that had Spain loaned them sufficient money with which to continue grinding, the men would have remained on the *centrals*, as the machine shops and residence of a sugar plantation are called, and that so few would have gone into the field against Spain that the insurrection could have been put down before it had gained headway. An advance to the sugar planters of five millions of dollars then, so they say, would have saved Spain the outlay of many hundreds of millions spent later in supporting an army in the field. That may or may not be true, and it is not important now, for Spain did not attack the insurgents in that way, but began hastily to build forts. These forts now, (1898), stretch all over the island, some in straight lines, some in circles, and some zig-zagging from hilltop to hilltop, some within a quarter of a mile of the next, and others so near that the sentries can toss a cartridge from one to the other.

The island is divided into two great military camps, one situated within the forts, and the other scattered over the fields and mountains outside of them. The Spaniards have absolute control over everything within the fortified places; that is, in all cities, towns, seaports, and along the lines of the railroad; the insurgents are in possession of all the rest. They are not in fixed possession, but they have control much as a mad bull may be said to have control of a ten-acre lot when he goes on the rampage. Some farmer may hold a legal right to the ten-acre lot, through title deeds or in the shape of a mortgage, and the bull may occupy but one part of it at a time, but he has possession, which is better than the law.

It is difficult to imagine a line drawn so closely, not about one city or town, but around every city and town in Cuba, that no one can pass the line from either the outside or the inside. The Spaniards, however, have succeeded in effecting and maintaining a blockade of that kind. They have placed forts next to the rows of houses or huts on the outskirts of each town, within a hundred yards of one another, and outside of this circle is another circle, and beyond that, on every high piece of ground, are still more of these little square forts, which are not much larger than the signal stations along the lines of our railroads and not unlike them in appearance. No one can cross the line of the forts without a pass, nor enter from the country beyond them without an order showing from what place he comes, at what time he left that place, and that he had permission from the *commandante* to leave it.

A stranger in any city in Cuba today is virtually in a prison, and is as isolated from the rest of the world as though he were on a desert island or a floating ship of war. When he wishes to depart he is free to do so, but he cannot leave on foot nor on horseback. He must make his departure on a railroad train, of which seldom more than two leave any town in twenty-four hours, one going east and the other west. From Havana a number of trains depart daily in different directions, but once outside of Havana, there is only one train back to it again. When on the cars you are still in the presence and under the care of Spanish soldiers, and the progress of the train is closely guarded. A pilot engine precedes it at a distance of one hundred yards to test the rails and pick up dynamite bombs, and in front of it is a car covered with armour plate, with slits in the sides like those in a letter box, through which the soldiers may fire. There are generally from twenty to fifty soldiers in each armoured car.

Back of the armoured car is a flat car loaded with ties, girders and rails, which are used to repair bridges or those portions of the track that may have been blown up by the insurgents. Wherever a track crosses a bridge there are two forts, one at each end of the bridge, and also at almost every cross-road. When the train passes one of these forts, two soldiers appear in the door and stand at salute to show, probably, that they are awake, and at every station there are two or more forts, while the stations themselves are usually protected by ramparts of ties and steel rails. There is no situation where it is so distinctly evident that those who are not with you are against you, for you are either inside of one circle of forts or passing under guard by rail to another circle, or you are with the insurgents. There is no alternative. If you walk fifty yards away from the circle you are, in the eyes of the Spaniards, as much in "the field" as though you were two hundred miles away on the mountains.

The lines are so closely drawn that when you consider the tremendous amount of time and labour expended in keeping up this blockade, you must admire the Spaniards for doing it so well, but you would admire them more, if, instead of stopping content with that they went further and invaded the field. The forts are an excellent precaution; they prevent sympathizers from joining the insurgents and from sending them food, arms, medicine or messages. But the next step, after blockading the cities, would appear to be to follow the insurgents into the field and give them battle. This the Spaniards do not seem to consider important, nor wish to do. Flying columns of regular troops and guerrillas are sent out daily, but they always return each evening within the circle of forts.

If they meet a band of insurgents, they give battle readily enough,

11

A Spanish Soldier

Young Spanish Officer

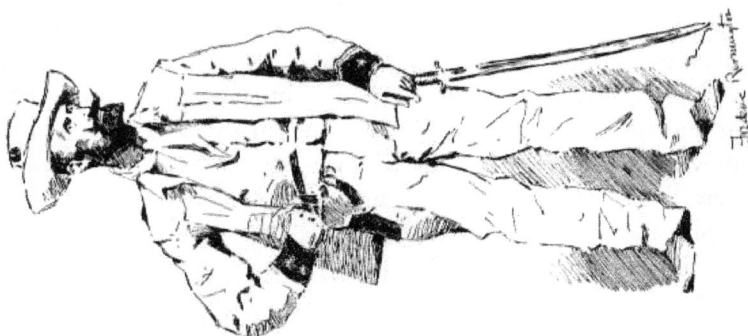

A Spanish Officer

but they never pursue the enemy, and, instead of camping on the ground and following him up the next morning, they retreat as soon as the battle is over, to the town where they are stationed. When occasionally objection is made to this by a superior officer, they give as an explanation that they were afraid of being led into an ambush, and that as an officer's first consideration must be for his men, they decided that it was wiser not to follow the enemy into what might prove a death-trap; or the officers say they could not abandon their wounded while they pursued the rebels. Sometimes a force of one thousand men will return with three men wounded, and will offer their condition as an excuse for having failed to follow the enemy.

About five years ago troops of United States cavalry were sent into the *chapparal* on the border of Mexico and Texas to drive the Garcia revolutionists back into their own country. One troop, G, Third Cavalry, was ordered out for seven days' service, but when I joined the troop later as a correspondent, it had been in the field for three months, sleeping the entire time under canvas, and carrying all its impedimenta with it on pack mules. It had seldom, if ever, been near a town, and the men wore the same clothes, or what was left of them, with which they had started for a week's campaign. Had the Spaniards followed such a plan of attack as that when the revolution began, instead of building mud forts and devastating the country, they might not only have suppressed the revolution, but the country would have been of some value when the war ended. As it is today, it will take ten years or more to bring it back to a condition of productiveness.

The wholesale devastation of the island was an idea of General Weyler's. If the captain of a vessel, in order to put down a mutiny on board, scuttled the ship and sent everybody to the bottom, his plan of action would be as successful as General Weyler's has proved to be. After he had obtained complete control of the cities, he decided to lay waste the country and starve the revolutionists into submission. So, he ordered all *pacíficos*, as the non-belligerents are called, into the towns and burned their houses, and issued orders to have all fields where potatoes or corn were planted dug up and these food products destroyed.

These *pacíficos* are now gathered inside of a dead line, drawn one hundred and fifty yards around the towns, or wherever there is a fort. Some of them have settled around the forts that guard a bridge, others around the forts that guard a sugar plantation; wherever there are forts there are *pacíficos*.

In a word, the situation in Cuba is something like this: The Span-

Guerillas With Captured Pacíficos

iards hold the towns, from which their troops daily make predatory raids, invariably returning in time for dinner at night. Around each town is a circle of *pacificos* doing no work, and for the most part starving and diseased, and outside, in the plains and mountains, are the insurgents. No one knows just where any one band of them is today or where it may be tomorrow. Sometimes they come up to the very walls of the fort, lasso a bunch of cattle and ride off again, and the next morning their presence may be detected ten miles away, where they are setting fire to a cane field or a sugar plantation.

This is the situation, so far as the inhabitants are concerned. The physical appearance of the country since the war began has changed greatly. In the days of peace Cuba was one of the most beautiful islands in the tropics, perhaps in the world. Its skies hang low and are brilliantly beautiful, with great expanses of blue, and in the early morning and before sunset, they are lighted with wonderful clouds of pink and saffron, as brilliant and as unreal as the fairy's grotto in a pantomime. There are great wind-swept prairies of high grass or tall sugarcane, and on the sea coast mountains of a light green, like the green of corroded copper, changing to a darker shade near the base, where they are covered with forests of palms.

Throughout the extent of the island run many little streams, sometimes between high banks of rock, covered with moss and magnificent fern, with great pools of clear, deep water at the base of high waterfalls, and in those places where the stream cuts its way through the level plains double rows of the royal palm mark its course. The royal palm is the characteristic feature of the landscape in Cuba. It is the most beautiful of all palms, and possibly the most beautiful of all trees.

The cocoanut palm, as one sees it in Egypt, picturesque as it is, has a pathetic resemblance to a shabby feather duster, and its trunk bends and twists as though it had not the strength to push its way through the air, and to hold itself erect. But the royal palm shoots up boldly from the earth with the grace and symmetry of a marble pillar or the white mast of a great ship. Its trunk swells in the centre and grows smaller again at the top, where it is hidden by great bunches of green plumes, like monstrous ostrich feathers that wave and bow and bend in the breeze as do the plumes on the head of a beautiful woman. Standing isolated in an open plain or in ranks in a forest of palms, this tree is always beautiful, noble and full of meaning. It makes you forget the ugly iron chimneys of the *centrals*, and it is the first and the last feature that appeals to the visitor in Cuba.

15

But since the revolution came to Cuba the beauty of the landscape is blotted with the grim and pitiable signs of war. The sugarcane has turned to a dirty brown where the fire has passed through it, the *centrals* are black ruins, and the *adobe* houses and the railroad stations are roofless, and their broken windows stare pathetically at you like blind eyes. War cannot alter the sunshine, but the smoke from the burning huts and the blazing cornfields seems all the more sad and terrible when it rises into such an atmosphere, and against so soft and beautiful a sky.

People frequently ask how far the destruction of property in Cuba is apparent. It is so far apparent that the smoke of burning buildings is seldom absent from the landscape. If you stand on an elevation it is possible to see from ten to twenty blazing houses, and the smoke from the cane fields creeping across the plain or rising slowly to meet the sky. Sometimes the train passes for hours through burning districts, and the heat from the fields along the track is so intense that it is impossible to keep the windows up, and whenever the door is opened sparks and cinders sweep into the car. One morning, just this side of Jovellanos, all the sugarcane on the right side of the track was wrapped in white smoke for miles so that nothing could be distinguished from that side of the car, and we seemed to be moving through the white steam of a Russian bath.

The Spaniards are no more to blame for this than are the insurgents; each destroy property and burn the cane. When an insurgent column finds a field planted with potatoes, it takes as much of the crop as it can carry away and chops up the remainder with machetes, to prevent it from falling into the hands of the Spaniards. If the Spaniards pass first, they act in exactly the same way.

Cane is not completely destroyed if it is burned, for if it is at once cut down just above the roots, it will grow again. When peace is declared it will not be the soil that will be found wanting, nor the sun. It will be the lack of money and the loss of credit that will keep the sugar planters from sowing and grinding. And the loss of machinery in the *centrals*, which is worth in single instances hundreds of thousands of dollars, and in the aggregate many millions, cannot be replaced by men, who, even when their machinery was intact, were on the brink of ruin.

Unless the United States Government interferes on account of some one of its citizens in Cuba, and war is declared with Spain, there is no saying how long the present revolution may continue. For the Spaniards themselves are acting in a way which makes many people suspect that they are not making an effort to bring it to an end. The

16

sincerity of the Spaniards in Spain is beyond question; the personal sacrifices they made in taking up the loans issued by the government are proof of their loyalty. But the Spaniards in Cuba are acting for their own interests. Many of the planters in order to save their fields and *centrals* from destruction, are unquestionably aiding the insurgents in secret, and though they shout "*Viva España*" in the cities, they pay out cartridges and money at the back door of their plantations.

It was because Weyler suspected that they were playing this double game that he issued secret orders that there should be no more grinding. For he knew that the same men who bribed him to allow them to grind would also pay blackmail to the insurgents for a like permission. He did not dare openly to forbid the grinding, but he instructed his officers in the field to visit those places where grinding was in progress and to stop it by some indirect means, such as by declaring that the laborers employed were suspects, or by seizing all the draught oxen ostensibly for the use of his army, or by insisting that the men employed must show a fresh permit to work every day, which could only be issued to them by some *commandante* stationed not less than ten miles distant from the plantation on which they were employed.

And the Spanish officers, as well as the planters—the very men to whom Spain looks to end the rebellion—are chief among those who are keeping it alive. The reasons for their doing so are obvious; they receive double pay while they are on foreign service, whether they are fighting or not, promotion comes twice as quickly as in time of peace, and orders and crosses are distributed by the gross. They are also able to make small fortunes out of forced loans from planters and suspects, and they undoubtedly hold back for themselves a great part of the pay of the men.

A certain class of Spanish officer has a strange sense of honour. He does not consider that robbing his government by falsifying his accounts, or by making incorrect returns of his expenses, is disloyal or unpatriotic. He holds such an act as lightly as many people do smuggling cigars through their own custom house, or robbing a corporation of a railroad fare. He might be perfectly willing to die for his country, but should he be permitted to live he will not hesitate to rob her.

A lieutenant, for instance, will take twenty men out for their daily walk through the surrounding country and after burning a few huts and butchering a *pacifico* or two, will come back in time for dinner and charge his captain for rations for fifty men and for three thousand cartridges "expended in service." The captain *vises* his report, and the two share the profits. Or they turn the money over to the colonel, who recommends them for red enamelled crosses for "bravery on the field." The only store in Matanzas that was doing a brisk trade when I was there was a jewellery shop, where they had sold more diamonds and watches to the Spanish officers since the revolution broke out than they had ever been able to dispose of before to all the rich men in the city. The legitimate pay of the highest ranking officer is barely enough to buy red wine for his dinner, certainly not enough to pay for champagne and diamonds; so it is not unfair to suppose that the rebellion is a profitable experience for the officers, and they have no intention of losing the golden eggs.

And the insurgents on the other side are equally determined to continue the conflict. From every point of view this is all that is left for them to do. They know by terrible experience how little of mercy or even of justice they may expect from the enemy, and, patriotism or the love of independence aside, it is better for them to die in the field than to risk the other alternative; a lingering life in an African penal settlement or the fusillade against the east wall of Cabañas prison. In an island with a soil so rich and productive as is that of Cuba there will always be roots and fruits for the insurgents to live upon, and with the cattle that they have hidden away in the laurel or on the mountains they can keep their troops in rations for an indefinite period. What they most need now are cartridges and rifles. Of men they have already more than they can arm.

People in the United States frequently express impatience at the small amount of fighting which takes place in this struggle for liberty, and it is true that the lists of killed show that the death rate in battle is inconsiderable. Indeed, when compared with the number of men and women who die daily of smallpox and fever and those who are butchered on the plantations, the proportion of killed in battle is probably about one to fifteen.

I have no statistics to prove these figures, but, judging from the hospital reports and from what the consuls tell of the many murders of *pacificos*, I judge that that proportion would be rather under than above the truth. George Bronson Rae, the *Herald* correspondent, who was for nine months with Maceo and Gomez, and who saw eighty fights and was twice wounded, told me that the largest number of insurgents he had seen killed in one battle was thirteen.

Another correspondent said that a Spanish officer had told him that he had killed forty insurgents out of four hundred who had at-

Insurgents Firing on a Spanish Fort

"One Shot for a Hundred"

tacked his column.

"But how do you know you killed that many?" the correspondent asked. "You say you were never nearer than half a mile to them, and that you fell back into the town as soon as they ceased firing."

"Ah, but I counted the cartridges my men had used," the officer replied. "I found they had expended four hundred. By allowing ten bullets to each man killed, I was able to learn that we had killed forty men."

These stories show how little reason there is to speak of these skirmishes as battles, and it also throws some light on the Spaniard's idea of his own marksmanship. As a plain statement of fact, and without any exaggeration, one of the chief reasons why half the insurgents in Cuba are not dead today is because the Spanish soldiers cannot shoot well enough to hit them. The Mauser rifle, which is used by all the Spanish soldiers, with the exception of the *Guardia Civile*, is a most excellent weapon for those who like clean, gentlemanly warfare, in which the object is to wound or to kill outright, and not to "shock" the enemy nor to tear his flesh in pieces. The weapon has hardly any trajectory up to one thousand yards, but, in spite of its precision, it is as useless in the hands of a guerrilla or the average Spanish soldier as a bow and arrow would be.

The fact that when the Spaniards say "within gunfire of the forts" they mean within one hundred and fifty yards of them shows how they estimate their own skill. Major Grover Flint, the *Journal* correspondent, told me of a fight that he witnessed in which the Spaniards fired two thousand rounds at forty insurgents only two hundred yards away, and only succeeded in wounding three of them. Sylvester Scovel once explained this bad marksmanship to me by pointing out that to shift the cartridge in a Mauser, it is necessary to hold the rifle at an almost perpendicular angle, and close up under the shoulder.

After the fresh cartridge has gone home the temptation to bring the butt to the shoulder before the barrel is level is too great for the Spanish Tommy, and, in his excitement, he fires most of his ammunition in the air over the heads of the enemy. He also fires so recklessly and rapidly that his gun often becomes too hot for him to handle it properly, and it is not an unusual sight to see him rest the butt on the ground and pull the trigger while the gun is in that position.

On the whole, the Spanish soldiers during this war in Cuba have contributed little to the information of those who are interested in military science. The tactics which the officers follow are those which were found effective at the battle of Waterloo, and in the Peninsular campaign. When attacked from an ambush a Spanish column forms at once into a hollow square, with the cavalry in the centre, and the firing is done in platoons. They know nothing of "open order," or of firing in skirmish line. If the Cubans were only a little better marksmen than their enemies they should, with such a target as a square furnishes them, kill about ten men where they now wound one.

With the war conducted under the conditions described here, there does not seem to be much promise of its coming to any immediate end unless some power will interfere. The Spaniards will probably continue to remain inside their forts, and the officers will continue to pay themselves well out of the rebellion.

And, on the other hand, the insurgents who call themselves rich when they have three cartridges, as opposed to the one hundred and fifty cartridges that every Spanish soldier carries, will probably very wisely continue to refuse to force the issue in any one battle.

Fire and Sword in Cuba

The Fate of the Pacificos

As is already well known in the United States, General Weyler issued an order some months ago commanding the country people living in the provinces of Pinar del Rio, Havana and Matanzas to betake themselves with their belongings to the fortified towns. His object in doing this was to prevent the *pacificos* from giving help to the insurgents, and from sheltering them and the wounded in their huts. So, flying columns of guerrillas and Spanish soldiers were sent to burn these huts, and to drive the inhabitants into the suburbs of the cities. When I arrived in Cuba sufficient time had passed for me to note the effects of this order, and to study the results as they are to be found in the provinces of Havana, Matanzas and Santa Clara, the order having been extended to embrace the latter province.

It looked then as though General Weyler was reaping what he had sown, and was face to face with a problem of his own creating. As far as a visitor could judge, the results of this famous order seemed to furnish a better argument to those who think the United States should interfere in behalf of Cuba, than did the fact that men were being killed there, and that both sides were devastating the island and wrecking property worth millions of dollars.

The order, apart from being unprecedented in warfare, proved an exceedingly short-sighted one, and acted almost immediately after the manner of a boomerang. The able-bodied men of each family who had remained loyal or at least neutral, so long as they were permitted to live undisturbed on their few acres, were not content to exist on the charity of a city, and they swarmed over to the insurgent ranks by the hundreds, and it was only the old and infirm and the women and children who went into the towns, where they at once became a burden on the Spanish residents, who were already distressed by the lack of trade and the high prices asked for food.

The order failed also in its original object of embarrassing the insurgents, for they are used to living out of doors and to finding food for themselves, and the destruction of the huts where they had been made welcome was not a great loss to men who, in a few minutes, with the aid of a machete, can construct a shelter from a palm tree.

So, the order failed to distress those against whom it was aimed, but brought swift and terrible suffering to those who were and are absolutely innocent of any intent against the government, as well as to the adherents of the government.

It is easy to imagine what happened when hundreds of people, in some towns thousands, were herded together on the bare ground, with no food, with no knowledge of sanitation, with no covering for their heads but palm leaves, with no privacy for the women and young girls, with no thought but as to how they could live until tomorrow.

It is true that in the country, also, these people had no covering for their huts but palm leaves, but those huts were made stoutly to endure. When a man built one of them he was building his home, not a shelter tent, and they were placed well apart from one another, with the free air of the plain or mountain blowing about them, with room for the sun to beat down and drink up the impurities, and with patches of green things growing in rows over the few acres. I have seen them like that all over Cuba, and I am sure that no disease could have sprung from houses built so admirably to admit the sun and the air.

I have also seen them, I might add in parenthesis, rising in sluggish columns of black smoke against the sky, hundreds of them, while those who had lived in them for years stood huddled together at a distance, watching the flames run over the dry rafters of their homes, roaring and crackling with delight, like something human or inhuman, and marring the beautiful sunlit landscape with great blotches of red flames.

The huts in which these people live at present lean one against the other, and there are no broad roads nor green tobacco patches to separate one from another. There are, on the contrary, only narrow paths, two feet wide, where dogs and cattle and human beings tramp over daily growing heaps of refuse and garbage and filth, and where malaria rises at night in a white winding sheet of poisonous mist.

The condition of these people differs in degree; some are living the life of gypsies, others are as destitute as so many shipwrecked emigrants, and still others find it difficult to hold up their heads and breathe.

24

A Spanish Guerrilla

An Officer of Spanish Guerillas

In Jaruco, in the Havana province, a town of only two thousand inhabitants, the deaths from smallpox averaged seven a day for the month of December, and while Frederic Remington and I were there, six victims of smallpox were carried past us up the hill to the burying ground in the space of twelve hours. There were Spanish soldiers as well as *pacíficos* among these, for the Spanish officers either know or care nothing about the health of their men.

There is no attempt made to police these military camps, and in Jaruco the filth covered the streets and the *plaza* ankle-deep, and even filled the corners of the church which had been turned into a fort, and had hammocks swung from the altars. The huts of the *pacíficos*, with from four to six people in each, were jammed together in rows a quarter of a mile long, within ten feet of the cavalry barracks, where sixty men and horses had lived for a month. Next to the stables were the barracks. No one was vaccinated, no one was clean, and all of them were living on half rations.

Jaruco was a little worse than the other towns, but I found that the condition of the people is about the same everywhere. Around every town and even around the forts outside of the towns, you will see from one hundred to five hundred of these palm huts, with the people crouched about them, covered with rags, starving, with no chance to obtain work.

In the city of Matanzas the huts have been built upon a hill, and so far neither smallpox nor yellow fever has made headway there; but there is nothing for these people to eat, either, and while I was there three babies died from plain, old-fashioned starvation and no other cause.

The government's report for the year just ended gives the number of deaths in three hospitals of Matanzas as three hundred and eighty for the year, which is an average of a little over one death a day. As a matter of fact, in the military hospital alone the soldiers during several months of last year died at the rate of sixteen a day. It seems hard that Spain should hold Cuba at such a sacrifice of her own people.

In Cardenas, one of the principal seaport towns of the island, I found the *pacíficos* lodged in huts at the back of the town and also in abandoned warehouses along the water front. The condition of these latter was so pitiable that it is difficult to describe it correctly and hope to be believed.

The warehouses are built on wooden posts about fifty feet from the water's edge. They were originally nearly as large in extent as Madison Square Garden, but the half of the roof of one has fallen in, carrying the flooring with it, and the *adobe* walls and one side of the sloping roof and the high wooden piles on which half of the floor once rested are all that remain.

Some time ago an unusually high tide swept in under one of these warehouses and left a pool of water a hundred yards long and as many wide, around the wooden posts, and it has remained there undisturbed. This pool is now covered a half-inch thick with green slime, coloured blue and yellow, and with a damp fungus spread over the wooden posts and up the sides of the walls.

Over this sewage are now living three hundred women and children and a few men. The floor beneath them has rotted away, and the planks have broken and fallen into the pool, leaving big gaps, through which rise day and night deadly stenches and poisonous exhalations from the pool below.

The people above it are not ignorant of their situation. They know that they are living over a death-trap, but there is no other place for them. Bands of guerrillas and flying columns have driven them in like sheep to this city, and, with no money and no chance to obtain work, they have taken shelter in the only place that is left open to them.

With planks and blankets and bits of old sheet iron they have, for the sake of decency, put up barriers across these abandoned warehouses, and there they are now sitting on the floor or stretched on heaps of rags, gaunt and hollow-eyed. Outside, in the angles of the fallen walls, and among the refuse of the warehouses, they have built fireplaces, and, with the few pots and kettles they use in common, they cook what food the children can find or beg.

One gentleman of Cardenas told me that a hundred of these people called at his house every day for a bit of food.

Old negroes and little white children, some of them as beautiful, in spite of their rags, as any children I ever saw, act as providers for this hapless colony. They beg the food and gather the sticks and do the cooking. Inside the old women and young mothers sit on the rotten planks listless and silent, staring ahead of them at nothing.

I saw the survivors of the Johnstown flood when the horror of that disaster was still plainly written in their eyes, but destitute as they were of home and food and clothing, they were in better plight than those fever-stricken, starving *pacíficos*, who have sinned in no way, who have given no aid to the rebels, and whose only crime is that they lived in the country instead of in the town. They are now to suffer because General Weyler, finding that he cannot hold the country as he

Murdering the Cuban Wounded

can the towns, lays it waste and treats those who lived there with less consideration than the Sultan of Morocco shows to the murderers in his jail at Tangier. Had these people been guilty of the most unnatural crimes, their punishment could not have been more severe nor their end more certain.

I found the hospital for this colony behind three blankets which had been hung across a corner of the warehouse. A young woman and a man were lying side by side, the girl on a cot and the man on the floor. The others sat within a few feet of them on the other side of the blankets, apparently lost to all sense of their danger, and too dejected and hopeless to even raise their eyes when I gave them money.

A fat little doctor was caring for the sick woman, and he pointed through the cracks in the floor at the green slime below us, and held his fingers to his nose and shrugged his shoulders. I asked him what ailed his patients, and he said it was yellow fever, and pointed again at the slime, which moved and bubbled in the hot sun.

He showed me babies with the skin drawn so tightly over their little bodies that the bones showed through as plainly as the rings under a glove. They were covered with sores, and they protested as loudly as they could against the treatment which the world was giving them, clinching their fists and sobbing with pain when the sore places came in contact with their mothers' arms. A planter who had at one time employed a large number of these people, and who was moving about among them, said that five hundred had died in Cardenas since the order to leave the fields had been issued. Another gentleman told me that in the huts at the back of the town there had been twenty-five cases of smallpox in one week of which seventeen had resulted in death.

I do not know that the United States will interfere in the affairs of Cuba, but whatever may happen later, this is what is likely to happen now, and it should have some weight in helping to decide the question with those whose proper business it is to determine it.

Thousands of human beings are now herded together around the seaport towns of Cuba who cannot be fed, who have no knowledge of cleanliness or sanitation, who have no doctors to care for them and who cannot care for themselves.

Many of them are dying of sickness and some of starvation, and this is the healthy season. In April and May the rains will come, and the fever will thrive and spread, and cholera, yellow fever and small-pox will turn Cuba into one huge plague spot, and the farmers' sons

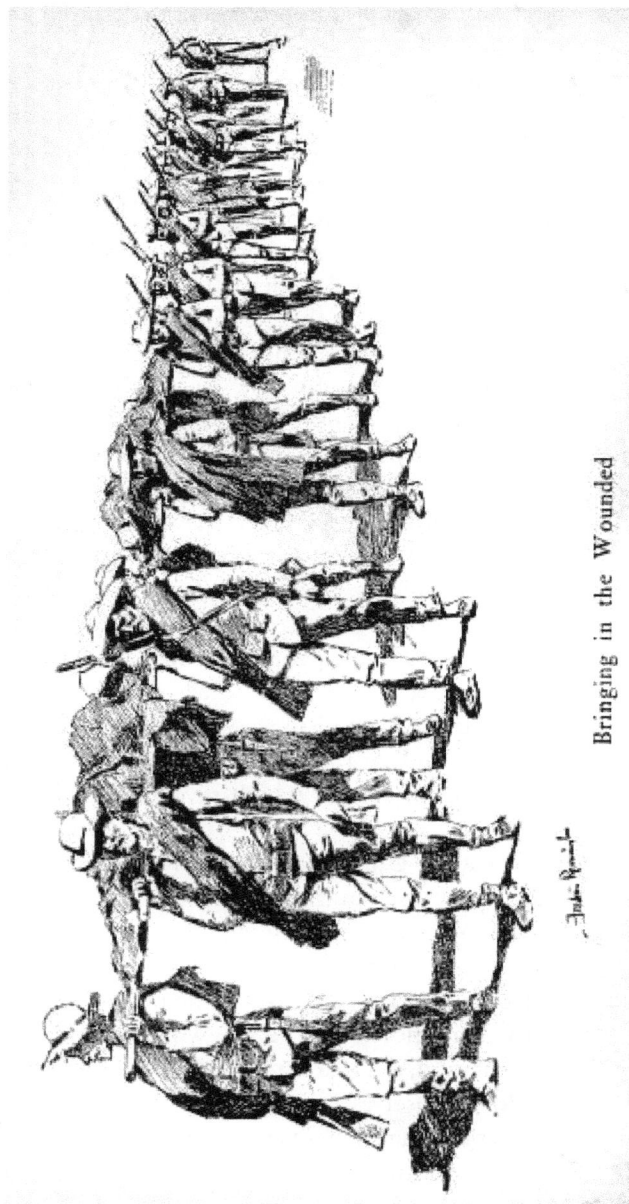

Bringing in the Wounded

whom Spain has sent over here to be soldiers, and who are dying by the dozens before they have learned to pull the comb off a bunch of cartridges, are going to die by the hundreds, and women and children who are innocent of any offense will die with them, and there will be a quarantine against Cuba, and no vessel can come into her ports or leave them.

All this is going to happen, I am led to believe, not from what I saw in any one village, but in hundreds of villages. It will not do to put it aside by saying that "War is war," and that "All war is cruel," or to ask, "Am I my brother's keeper?"

In other wars men have fought with men, and women have suffered indirectly because the men were killed, but in this war it is the women, herded together in the towns like cattle, who are going to die, while the men, camped in the fields and the mountains, will live.

It is a situation which charity might help to better, but in any event, it is a condition which deserves the most serious consideration from men of common sense and judgment, and one not to be treated with hysterical headlines nor put aside as a necessary evil of war.

The Death of Rodriguez

Adolfo Rodríguez was the only son of a Cuban farmer, who lives nine miles outside of Santa Clara, beyond the hills that surround that city to the north.

When the revolution broke out young Rodríguez joined the insurgents, leaving his father and mother and two sisters at the farm. He was taken, in December of 1896, by a force of the *Guardia Civile*, the *corps d'élite* of the Spanish Army, and defended himself when they tried to capture him, wounding three of them with his machete.

He was tried by a military court for bearing arms against the government, and sentenced to be shot by a fusillade some morning, before sunrise.

Previous to execution, he was confined in the military prison of Santa Clara, with thirty other insurgents, all of whom were sentenced to be shot, one after the other, on mornings following the execution of Rodríguez.

His execution took place the morning of the 19th of January, at a place a half-mile distant from the city, on the great plain that stretches from the forts out to the hills, beyond which Rodríguez had lived for nineteen years. At the time of his death he was twenty years old.

I witnessed his execution, and what follows is an account of the way he went to death. The young man's friends could not be present, for it was impossible for them to show themselves in that crowd and that place with wisdom or without distress, and I like to think that, although Rodríguez could not know it, there was one person present when he died who felt keenly for him, and who was a sympathetic though unwilling spectator.

There had been a full moon the night preceding the execution, and when the squad of soldiers marched out from town it was still shining brightly through the mists, although it was past five o'clock.

It lighted a plain two miles in extent broken by ridges and gullies and covered with thick, high grass and with bunches of cactus and *palmetto*. In the hollow of the ridges the mist lay like broad lakes of water, and on one side of the plain stood the walls of the old town. On the other rose hills covered with royal palms that showed white in the moonlight, like hundreds of marble columns. A line of tiny camp fires that the sentries had built during the night stretched between the forts at regular intervals and burned brightly.

But as the light grew stronger, and the moonlight faded, these were stamped out, and when the soldiers came in force the moon was a white ball in the sky, without radiance, the fires had sunk to ashes, and the sun had not yet risen.

So, even when the men were formed into three sides of a hollow square, they were scarcely able to distinguish one another in the uncertain light of the morning.

There were about three hundred soldiers in the formation. They belonged to the Volunteers, and they deployed upon the plain with their band in front, playing a jaunty quickstep, while their officers galloped from one side to the other through the grass, seeking out a suitable place for the execution, while the band outside the line still played merrily.

A few men and boys, who had been dragged out of their beds by the music, moved about the ridges, behind the soldiers, half-clothed, unshaven, sleepy-eyed, yawning and stretching themselves nervously and shivering in the cool, damp air of the morning.

Either owing to discipline or on account of the nature of their errand or because the men were still but half awake, there was no talking in the ranks, and the soldiers stood motionless, leaning on their rifles, with their backs turned to the town, looking out across the plain to the hills.

The men in the crowd behind them were also grimly silent. They knew that whatever they might say would be twisted into a word of sympathy for the condemned man or a protest against the government. So, no one spoke; even the officers gave their orders in gruff whispers, and the men in the crowd did not mix together, but looked suspiciously at one another and kept apart.

As the light increased a mass of people came hurrying from the town with two black figures leading them, and the soldiers drew up at attention, and part of the double line fell back and left an opening in the square.

With us a condemned man walks only the short distance from his cell to the scaffold or the electric chair, shielded from sight by the prison walls; and it often occurs even then that the short journey is too much for his strength and courage.

But the merciful Spaniards on this morning made the prisoner walk for over a half-mile across the broken surface of the fields. I expected to find the man, no matter what his strength at other times might be, stumbling and faltering on this cruel journey, but as he came nearer I saw that he led all the others, that the priests on either side of him were taking two steps to his one, and that they were tripping on their gowns and stumbling over the hollows, in their efforts to keep pace with him as he walked, erect and soldierly, at a quick step in advance of them.

He had a handsome, gentle face of the peasant type, a light, pointed beard, great wistful eyes and a mass of curly black hair. He was shockingly young for such a sacrifice, and looked more like a Neapolitan than a Cuban. You could imagine him sitting on the quay at Naples or Genoa, lolling in the sun and showing his white teeth when he laughed. He wore a new *scapula* around his neck, hanging outside his linen blouse.

It seems a petty thing to have been pleased with at such a time, but I confess to have felt a thrill of satisfaction when I saw, as the Cuban passed me, that he held a cigarette between his lips, not arrogantly nor with bravado, but with the nonchalance of a man who meets his punishment fearlessly, and who will let his enemies see that they can kill but cannot frighten him.

It was very quickly finished, with rough, and, but for one frightful blunder, with merciful swiftness. The crowd fell back when it came to the square, and the condemned man, the priests and the firing squad of six young volunteers passed in and the line closed behind them.

The officer who had held the cord that bound the Cuban's arms behind him and passed across his breast, let it fall on the grass and drew his sword, and Rodriguez dropped his cigarette from his lips and bent and kissed the cross which the priest held up before him.

The elder of the priests moved to one side and prayed rapidly in a loud whisper, while the other, a younger man, walked away behind the firing squad and covered his face with his hands and turned his back. They had both spent the last twelve hours with Rodriguez in the chapel of the prison.

The Cuban walked to where the officer directed him to stand, and

The Death of Rodriguez

turned his back to the square and faced the hills and the road across them which led to his father's farm.

As the officer gave the first command, he straightened himself as far as the cords would allow, and held up his head and fixed his eyes immovably on the morning light which had just begun to show above the hills.

He made a picture of such pathetic helplessness, but of such courage and dignity, that he reminded me on the instant of that statue of Nathan Hale, which stands in the City Hall Park, above the roar of Broadway, and teaches a lesson daily to the hurrying crowds of money-makers who pass beneath.

The Cuban's arms were bound, as are those of the statue, and he stood firmly, with his weight resting on his heels like a soldier on parade, and with his face held up fearlessly, as is that of the statue. But there was this difference, that Rodriguez, while probably as willing to give six lives for his country as was the American rebel, being only a peasant, did not think to say so, and he will not, in consequence, live in bronze during the lives of many men, but will be remembered only as one of thirty Cubans, one of whom was shot at Santa Clara on each succeeding day at sunrise.

The officer had given the order, the men had raised their pieces, and the condemned man had heard the clicks of the triggers as they were pulled back, and he had not moved. And then happened one of the most cruelly refined, though unintentional, acts of torture that one can very well imagine. As the officer slowly raised his sword, preparatory to giving the signal, one of the mounted officers rode up to him and pointed out silently what I had already observed with some satisfaction, that the firing squad were so placed that when they fired they would shoot several of the soldiers stationed on the extreme end of the square.

Their captain motioned his men to lower their pieces, and then walked across the grass and laid his hand on the shoulder of the waiting prisoner.

It is not pleasant to think what that shock must have been. The man had steeled himself to receive a volley of bullets in his back. He believed that in the next instant he would be in another world; he had heard the command given, had heard the click of the Mausers as the locks caught—and then, at that supreme moment, a human hand had been laid upon his shoulder and a voice spoke in his ear.

You would expect that any man who had been snatched back to

36

The Cuban Martyrdom

life in such a fashion would start and tremble at the reprieve, or would break down altogether, but this boy turned his head steadily, and followed with his eyes the direction of the officer's sword, then nodded his head gravely, and, with his shoulders squared, took up a new position, straightened his back again, and once more held himself erect.

As an exhibition of self-control this should surely rank above feats of heroism performed in battle, where there are thousands of comrades to give inspiration. This man was alone, in the sight of the hills he knew, with only enemies about him, with no source to draw on for strength but that which lay within himself.

The officer of the firing squad, mortified by his blunder, hastily whipped up his sword, the men once more levelled their rifles, the sword rose, dropped, and the men fired. At the report the Cuban's head snapped back almost between his shoulders, but his body fell slowly, as though someone had pushed him gently forward from behind and he had stumbled.

He sank on his side in the wet grass without a struggle or sound, and did not move again.

It was difficult to believe that he meant to lie there, that it could be ended so without a word, that the man in the linen suit would not get up on his feet and continue to walk on over the hills, as he apparently had started to do, to his home; that there was not a mistake somewhere, or that at least some one would be sorry or say something or run to pick him up.

But, fortunately, he did not need help, and the priests returned—the younger one, with the tears running down his face—and donned their vestments and read a brief requiem for his soul, while the squad stood uncovered, and the men in hollow square shook their accoutrements into place, and shifted their pieces and got ready for the order to march, and the band began again with the same quickstep which the fusillade had interrupted.

The figure still lay on the grass untouched, and no one seemed to remember that it had walked there of itself, or noticed that the cigarette still burned, a tiny ring of living fire, at the place where the figure had first stood.

The figure was a thing of the past, and the squad shook itself like a great snake, and then broke into little pieces and started off jauntily, stumbling in the high grass and striving to keep step to the music.

The officers led it past the figure in the linen suit, and so close to it that the file closers had to part with the column to avoid treading on it. Each soldier as he passed turned and looked down on it, some craning their necks curiously, others giving a careless glance, and some without any interest at all, as they would have looked at a house by the roadside or a passing cart or a hole in the road.

One young soldier caught his foot in a trailing vine, and fell forward just opposite to it. He grew very red when his comrades giggled at him for his awkwardness. The crowd of sleepy spectators fell in on either side of the band. They had forgotten it, too, and the priests put their vestments back in the bag and wrapped their heavy cloaks about them, and hurried off after the others.

Everyone seemed to have forgotten it except two men, who came slowly toward it from the town, driving a bullock cart that bore an unplaned coffin, each with a cigarette between his lips, and with his throat wrapped in a shawl to keep out the morning mists.

At that moment the sun, which had shown some promise of its coming in the glow above the hills, shot up suddenly from behind them in all the splendour of the tropics, a fierce, red disc of heat, and filled the air with warmth and light.

The bayonets of the retreating column flashed in it, and at the sight of it a rooster in a farmyard nearby crowed vigorously and a dozen bugles answered the challenge with the brisk, cheery notes of the reveille, and from all parts of the city the church bells jangled out the call for early mass, and the whole world of Santa Clara seemed to stir and stretch itself and to wake to welcome the day just begun.

But as I fell in at the rear of the procession and looked back the figure of the young Cuban, who was no longer a part of the world of Santa Clara, was asleep in the wet grass, with his motionless arms still tightly bound behind him, with the scapula twisted awry across his face and the blood from his breast sinking into the soil he had tried to free.

Regular Cavalryman—Spanish

Spanish Cavalryman on a Texas Broncho

Along the Trocha

This is an account of a voyage of discovery along the Spanish *tro-cha*, the one at the eastern end of Cuba. It is the longer of the two, and stretches from coast to coast at the narrowest part of that half of the island, from Jucaro on the south to Moron on the north.

Before I came to Cuba this time, I had read in our newspapers about the Spanish *trocha* without knowing just what a *trocha* was. I imagined it to be a rampart of earth and fallen trees, topped with barbed wire; a Rubicon that no one was allowed to pass, but which the insurgents apparently crossed at will with the ease of little girls leaping over a flying skipping rope. In reality it seems to be a much more important piece of engineering than is generally supposed, and one which, when completed, may prove an absolute barrier to the progress of large bodies of troops unless they are supplied with artillery.

I saw twenty-five of its fifty miles, and the engineers in charge told me that I was the first American, or foreigner of any nationality, who had been allowed to visit it and make drawings and photographs of it. Why they allowed me to see it I do not know, nor can I imagine either why they should have objected to my doing so. There is no great mystery about it.

Indeed, what impressed me most concerning it was the fact that every bit of material used in constructing this backbone of the Spanish defence, this strategic point of all their operations, and their chief hope of success against the revolutionists, was furnished by their despised and hated enemies in the United States. Every sheet of armour plate, every corrugated zinc roof, every roll of barbed wire, every plank, beam, rafter and girder, even the nails that hold the planks together, the forts themselves, shipped in sections, which are numbered in readiness for setting up, the ties for the military railroad which clings to the *trocha* from one sea to the other—all of these have been

One of the Block Houses

From a photograph taken by Mr. Davis

supplied by manufacturers in the United States.

This is interesting when one remembers that the American in the Spanish illustrated papers is represented as a hog, and generally with the United States flag for trousers, and Spain as a noble and valiant lion. Yet it would appear that the lion is willing to save a few dollars on freight by buying his armament from his hoggish neighbour, and that the American who cheers for Cuba Libre is not at all averse to making as many dollars as he can in building the wall against which the Cubans may be eventually driven and shot.

If the insurgents have found as much difficulty in crossing the *trocha* by land as I found in reaching it by water, they are deserving of all sympathy as patient and long-suffering individuals.

A thick jungle stretches for miles on either side of the *trocha*, and the only way of reaching it from the outer world is through the seaports at either end. Of these, Moron is all but landlocked, and Jucaro is guarded by a chain of keys, which make it necessary to reship all the troops and their supplies and all the material for the *trocha* to lighters, which meet the vessels six miles out at sea.

A dirty Spanish steamer drifted with us for two nights and a day from Cienfuegos to Jucaro, and three hundred Spanish soldiers, dusty, ragged and barefooted, owned her as completely as though she had been a regular transport. They sprawled at full length over every deck, their guns were stacked in each corner, and their hammocks swung four deep from railings and riggings and across companionways, and even from the bridge itself. It was not possible to take a step without treading on one of them, and their hammocks made a walk on the deck something like a hurdle race.

With the soldiers, and crowding them for space, were the officers' mules and ponies, steers, calves and squealing pigs, while crates full of chickens were piled on top of one another as high as the hurricane deck, so that the roosters and the buglers vied with each other in continual contests. It was like traveling with a floating menagerie. Twice a day the bugles sounded the call for breakfast and dinner, and the soldiers ceased to sprawl, and squatted on the deck around square tin cans filled with soup or red wine, from which they fed themselves with spoons and into which they dipped their rations of hard tack, after first breaking them on the deck with a blow from a bayonet or crushing them with a rifle butt.

The steward brought what was supposed to be a sample of this soup to the officer seated in the pilot house high above the squalor, and he would pick out a bean from the mess on the end of a fork and place it to his lips and nod his head gravely, and the grinning steward would carry the dish away.

But the soldiers seemed to enjoy it very much, and to be content, even cheerful. There are many things to admire about the Spanish Tommy. In the seven fortified cities which I visited, where there were thousands of him, I never saw one drunk or aggressive, which is much more than you can say of his officers. On the march he is patient, eager and alert. He trudges from fifteen to thirty miles a day over the worst roads ever constructed by man, in canvas shoes with rope soles, carrying one hundred and fifty cartridges, fifty across his stomach and one hundred on his back, weighing in all fifty pounds.

With these he has his Mauser, his blanket and an extra pair of shoes, and as many tin plates and bottles and bananas and potatoes and loaves of white bread as he can stow away in his blouse and knapsack. And this under a sun which makes even a walking stick seem a burden. In spite of his officers, and not on account of them, he maintains good discipline, and no matter how tired he may be or how much he may wish to rest on his plank bed, he will always struggle to his feet when the officers pass, and stand at salute. He gets very little in return for his efforts.

One Sunday night, when the band was playing in the *plaza*, at a heaven-forsaken fever camp called Ciego de Avila, a group of soldiers were sitting near me on the grass enjoying the music. They loitered there a few minutes after the bugle had sounded the retreat to the barracks, and the officer of the day found them. When they stood up he ordered them to report themselves at the *cartel* under arrest, and then, losing all control of himself, lashed one little fellow over the head with his colonel's staff, while the boy stood with his eyes shut and with his lips pressed together, but holding his hand at salute until the officer's stick beat it down.

These soldiers are from the villages and towns of Spain; some of them are not more than seventeen years old, and they are not volunteers. They do not care whether Spain owns an island eighty miles from the United States, or loses it, but they go out to it and have their pay stolen, and are put to building earth forts and stone walls, and die of fever. It seems a poor return for their unconscious patriotism when a colonel thrashes one of them as though he were a dog, especially as he knows the soldier may not strike back.

The second night out the ship steward showed us a light lying low

Spanish Cavalry

From photographs taken by Mr. Davis

in the water, and told us that was Jucaro, and we accepted his statement and went over the side into an open boat, in which we drifted about until morning, while the coloured man who owned the boat, and a little mulatto boy who steered it, quarrelled as to where exactly the town of Jucaro might be. They brought us up at last against a dark shadow of a house, built on wooden posts, and apparently floating in the water. This was the town of Jucaro as seen at that hour of the night, and as we left it before sunrise the next morning, I did not know until my return whether I had slept in a stationary ark or on the end of a wharf.

We found four other men sleeping on the floor in the room assigned us, and outside, eating by a smoking candle, a young English boy, who looked up and laughed when he heard us speak, and said:

"You've come at last, have you? You are the first white men I've seen since I came here. That's twelve months ago."

He was the cable operator at Jucaro; and he sits all day in front of a sheet of white paper, and watches a ray of light play across an imaginary line, and he can tell by its quivering, so he says, all that is going on all over the world. Outside of his whitewashed cable office is the landlocked bay, filled with wooden piles to keep out the sharks, and back of him lies the village of Jucaro, consisting of two open places filled with green slime and filth and thirty huts. But the operator said that what with fishing and bathing and *Tit-Bits* and *Lloyd's Weekly Times,* Jucaro was quite enjoyable. He is going home the year after this.

"At least, that's how I put it," he explained. "My contract requires me to stop on here until December of 1898, but it doesn't sound so long if you say 'a year after this,' does it?" He had had the yellow fever, and had never, owing to the war, been outside of Jucaro. "Still," he added, "I'm seeing the world, and I've always wanted to visit foreign parts."

As one of the few clean persons I met in Cuba, and the only contented one, I hope the cable operator at Jucaro will get a rise in salary soon, and some day see more of foreign parts than he is seeing at present, and at last get back to "the Horse Shoe, at the corner of Tottenham Court Road and Oxford street, sir," where, as we agreed, better entertainment is to be had on Saturday night than anywhere in London.

In Havana, General Weyler had given me a pass to enter fortified places, which, except for the authority which the signature implied, meant nothing, as all the cities and towns in Cuba are fortified, and anyone can visit them. It was as though Mayor Strong had given a man a permit to ride in all the cable cars attached to cables.

One of the Forts Along the Trocha

From photograph taken by Mr. Davis

It was not intended to include the *trocha*, but I argued that if a *trocha* was not a "fortified place" nothing else was, and I persuaded the *commandante* at Jucaro to take that view of it and to *vise* Weyler's order. So at five the following morning a box car, with wooden planks stretched across it for seats, carried me along the line of the *trocha* from Jucaro to Ciego, the chief military port on the fortifications, and consumed five hot and stifling hours in covering twenty-five miles.

The *trocha* is a cleared space, one hundred and fifty to two hundred yards wide, which stretches for fifty miles through what is apparently an impassable jungle. The trees which have been cut down in clearing this passageway have been piled up at either side of the cleared space and laid in parallel rows, forming a barrier of tree trunks and roots and branches as wide as Broadway and higher than a man's head. It would take a man some time to pick his way over these barriers, and a horse could no more do it than it could cross a jam of floating logs in a river.

Between the fallen trees lies the single track of the military railroad, and on one side of that is the line of forts and a few feet beyond them a maze of barbed wire. Beyond the barbed wire again is he other barrier of fallen trees and the jungle. In its unfinished state this is not an insurmountable barricade. Gomez crossed it last November by daylight with six hundred men, and with but the loss of twenty-seven killed and as many wounded. Today it would be more difficult, and in a few months, without the aid of artillery, it will be impossible, except with the sacrifice of a great loss of life. The forts are of three kinds. They are best described as the forts, the blockhouses and the little forts. A big fort consists of two storeys, with a cellar below and a watch tower above. It is made of stone and *adobe*, and is painted a glaring white. One of these is placed at intervals of every half mile along the *trocha*, and on a clear day the sentry in the watch tower of each can see three forts on either side.

Midway between the big forts, at a distance of a quarter of a mile from each, is a blockhouse of two stories with the upper story of wood, overhanging the lower foundation of mud. These are placed at right angles to the railroad, instead of facing it, as do the forts.

Between each blockhouse and each fort are three little forts of mud and planks, surrounded by a ditch. They look something like a farmer's ice house as we see it at home, and they are about as hot inside as the other is cold. They hold five men, and are within hailing distance of one another. Back of them are three rows of stout wooden stakes, with barbed wire stretching from one row to the other, interlacing and crossing and running in and out above and below, like an intricate cat's cradle of wire.

One can judge how closely knit it is by the fact that to every twelve yards of posts there are four hundred and fifty yards of wire fencing. The forts are most completely equipped in their way, but twelve men in the jungle would find it quite easy to keep twelve men securely imprisoned in one of them for an indefinite length of time.

The walls are about twelve feet high, with a cellar below and a vault above the cellar. The roof of the vault forms a platform, around which the four walls rise to the height of a man's shoulder. There are loopholes for rifles in the sides of the vault, and where the platform joins the walls. These latter allow the men in the fort to fire down almost directly upon the head of anyone who comes up close to the wall of the fort, where, without these holes in the floor, it would be impossible to fire on him except by leaning far over the rampart.

Above the platform is an iron or zinc roof, supported by iron pillars, and in the centre of this is the watch tower. The only approach to the fort is by a movable ladder, which hangs over the side like the gangway of a ship of war, and can be raised by those on the inside by means of a rope suspended over a wheel in the roof. The opening in the wall at the head of the ladder is closed at the time of an attack by an iron platform, to which the ladder leads, and which also can be raised by a pulley. In October of 1897 the Spanish hope to have calcium lights placed in the watch towers of the forts with sufficient power to throw a searchlight over a quarter of a mile, or to the next blockhouse, and so keep the *trocha* as well lighted as Broadway from one end to the other.

As a further protection against the insurgents the Spaniards have distributed a number of bombs along the *trocha*, which they showed with great pride. These are placed at those points along the *trocha* where the jungle is less thickly grown, and where the insurgents might be expected to pass.

Each bomb is fitted with an explosive cap, to which five or six wires are attached and staked down on the ground. Any one stumbling over one of these wires explodes the bomb and throws a charge of broken iron to a distance of fifty feet. How the Spaniards are going to prevent stray cattle and their own soldiers from wandering into these man-traps it is difficult to understand.

The chief engineer in charge of the *trocha* detailed a captain to take me over it and to show me all that there was to see. The officers of

The Trocha

From a photograph taken by Mr. Davis

the infantry and cavalry stationed at Ciego objected to his doing this, but he said: "He has a pass from General Weyler. I am not responsible." It was true that I had an order from General Weyler, but he had rendered it ineffective by having me followed about wherever I went by his police and spies. They sat next to me in the *cafés* and in the *plazas*, and when I took a cab they called the next one on the line and trailed after mine all around the city, until my driver would become alarmed for fear he, too, was suspected of something, and would take me back to the hotel.

I had gotten rid of them at Cienfuegos by purchasing a ticket on the steamer to Santiago, three days further down the coast, and then dropping off in the night at the *trocha*, so while I was visiting it I expected to find that my non-arrival at Santiago had been reported, and word sent to the *trocha* that I was a newspaper correspondent. And whenever an officer spoke to the one who was showing me about, my camera appeared to grow to the size of a trunk, and to weigh like lead, and I felt lonely, and longed for the company of the cheerful cable operator at the other end of the *trocha*.

But as I had seen Mr. Gillette in "Secret Service" only seventeen times before leaving New York, I knew just what to do, which was to smoke all the time and keep cool. The latter requirement was somewhat difficult, as Ciego de Avila is a hotter place than Richmond. Indeed, I can only imagine one place hotter than Ciego, and I have not been there.

Ciego was an interesting town. During every day of the last rainy season an average of thirty soldiers and officers died there of yellow fever. While I was there I saw two soldiers, one quite an old man, drop down in the street as though they had been shot, and lie in the road until they were carried to the yellow fever ward of the hospital, under the black oilskin cloth of the stretchers.

There was a very smart officers' club at Ciego well supplied with a bar and billiard tables, which I made some excuse for not entering, but which could be seen through its open doors, and I suggested to one of the members that it must be a comfort to have such a place, where the officers might go after their day's march on the mud banks of the *trocha*, and where they could bathe and be cool and clean. He said there were no baths in the club nor anywhere in the town. He added that he thought it might be a good idea to have them.

The bath tub is the dividing line between savages and civilized beings. And when I learned that regiment after regiment of Spanish officers and gentlemen have been stationed in that town—and it was the dirtiest, hottest and dustiest town I ever visited—for eighteen months, and none of them had wanted a bath, I believed from that moment all the stories I had heard about their butcheries and atrocities, stories which I had verified later by more direct evidence.

From a military point of view the *trocha* impressed me as a weapon which could be made to cut both ways. What the Spaniards think of it is shown by the caricature which appeared lately in *Don Quixote*, and which shows the United States represented by a hog and the insurgents represented by a negro imprisoned in the *trocha*, while Weyler stands ready to turn the Spanish lion on them and watch it gobble them up.

It would be unkind were Spain to do anything so inconsiderate, and besides, the United States is rather a large mouthful even without the insurgents who taken alone seem to have given the lion some pangs of indigestion.

If the *trocha* were situated on a broad plain or prairie with a mile of clear ground on either side of it, where troops could manoeuvre, and which would prevent the enemy from stealing up to it unseen, it might be a useful line of defence. But at present, along its entire length, stretches this almost impassable barrier of jungle. Now suppose the troops are sent at short notice from the military camps along the line to protect any particular point?

Not less than a thousand soldiers must be sent forward, and one can imagine what their condition would be were they forced to manoeuvre in a space one hundred and fifty yards broad, the half of which is taken up with barbed wire fences, fallen trees and explosive bomb shells. Only two hundred at the most could find shelter in the forts, which would mean that eight hundred men would be left outside the breastworks and scattered over a distance of a half mile, with a forest on both sides of them, from which the enemy could fire volley after volley into their ranks, protected from pursuit not only by the jungle, but by the walls of fallen trees which the Spaniards themselves have placed there.

A *trocha* in an open plain, as were the English *trocha*s in the desert around Suakin, makes an admirable defence, when a few men are forced to withstand the assault of a great many, but fighting behind a *trocha* in a jungle is like fighting in an ambush, and if the *trocha* at Moron is ever attacked in force it will prove to be a Valley of Death to the Spanish troops.

Spanish Troops in Action

The Question of Atrocities

One of the questions that is most frequently asked of those who have been in Cuba is how much truth exists in the reports of Spanish butcheries. It is safe to say in answer to this that while the report of a particular atrocity may not be true, other atrocities just as horrible have occurred and nothing has been heard of them. I was somewhat sceptical of Spanish atrocities until I came to Cuba, chiefly because I had been kept sufficiently long in Key West to learn how large a proportion of Cuban war news is manufactured on the *piazzas* of the hotels of that town and of Tampa by utterly irresponsible newspaper men who accept every rumour that finds its way across the gulf, and pass these rumours on to some of the New York papers as facts coming direct from the field.

It is not surprising that one becomes sceptical, for if one story proves to be false, how is the reader to know that the others are not inventions also? It is difficult to believe, for instance, the account of a horrible butchery if you read in the paragraph above it that two correspondents have been taken prisoners by the Spanish, when both of these gentlemen are sitting beside you in Key West and are, to your certain knowledge, reading the paragraph over your shoulder. Nor is it unnatural that one should grow doubtful of reported Cuban victories if he reads of the taking of Santa Clara and the flight of the Spanish garrison from that city, when he is living at Santa Clara and cannot find a Cuban in it with sufficient temerity to assist him to get out of it through the Spanish lines.

But because a Jacksonville correspondent has invented the tale of one butchery, it is no reason why the people in the United States should dismiss all the others as sensational fictions. After I went to Cuba I refused for weeks to listen to tales of butcheries, because I did not believe in them and because there seemed to be no way of verifying them—those who had been butchered could not testify and their relatives were too fearful of the vengeance of the Spaniards to talk about what had befallen a brother or a father. But towards the end of my visit I went to Sagua la Grande and there met a number of Americans and Englishmen, concerning whose veracity there could be no question. What had happened to their friends and the labourers on their plantations was exactly what had happened and is happening today to other *pacíficos* all over the island.

Sagua la Grande is probably no worse a city than others in Cuba, but it has been rendered notorious by the presence in that city of the guerrilla chieftain, Benito Cerreros.

Early in last December *Leslie's Illustrated Weekly* published half-tone reproductions of two photographs which were taken in Sagua. One was a picture of the bodies of six Cuban *pacíficos* lying on their backs, with their arms and legs bound and their bodies showing mutilation by machetes, and their faces pounded and hacked out of resemblance to anything human. The other picture was of a group of Spanish guerrillas surrounding their leader, a little man with a heavy moustache. His face was quite as inhuman as the face of any of the dead men he had mutilated. It wore a satisfied smile of fatuous vanity, and of the most diabolical cruelty. No artist could have drawn a face from his imagination which would have been more cruel.

The letter press accompanying these photographs explained that this guerrilla leader, Benito Cerreros, had found six unarmed *pacíficos* working in a field near Sagua, and had murdered them and then brought their bodies in a cart to that town, and had paid the local photographer to take a picture of them and of himself and his body guard. He claimed that he had killed the Cubans in open battle, but was so stupid as to forget to first remove the ropes with which he had bound them before he shot them. The photographs told the story without any aid from the letter press, and it must have told it to a great many people, judging from the number who spoke of it.

It seemed as if, for the first time, something definite regarding the reported Spanish atrocities had been placed before the people of the United States, which they could see for themselves. I had this photograph in my mind when I came to Sagua, and on the night that I arrived there, by a coincidence, the townspeople were giving Cerreros a dinner to celebrate a fresh victory of his over two insurgents, a naturalised American and a native Cuban.

The American was visiting the Cuban in the field, and they were lying in hiding outside of the town in a hut. The Cuban, who was a colonel in the insurgent army, had captured a Spanish spy, but had given him his liberty on the condition that he would go into Sagua and bring back some medicines. The colonel was dying of consumption, but he hoped that, with proper medicine, he might remain alive a few months longer. The spy, instead of keeping his word, betrayed the hiding place of the Cuban and the American to Cerreros, who rode out by night to surprise them. He took with him thirty-two guerrillas, and, lest that might not be enough to protect him from two men, added twelve of the Guarda Civile to their number, making forty-four men in all. They surrounded the hut in which the Cuban and the American were concealed, and shot them through the window as they sat at a table in the light of a candle. They then hacked the bodies with machetes. It was in recognition of this victory that the banquet was tendered to Cerreros by admiring friends.

Civilized nations recognise but three methods of dealing with prisoners captured in war. They are either paroled or exchanged or put in prison; that is what was done with them in our rebellion. It is not allowable to shoot prisoners; at least it is not generally done when they are seated unconscious of danger at a table. It may be said, however, that, as these two men were in arms against the government, they were only suffering the punishment of their crime, and that this is not a good instance of an atrocity. There are, however, unfortunately, many other instances in which the victims were non-combatants and their death simply murder. But it is extremely difficult to tell convincingly of these cases, without giving names, and the giving of names might lead to more deaths in Sagua. It is also difficult to convince the reader of murders for which there seems to have been no possible object.

And yet Cerreros and other guerrillas are murdering men and boys in the fields around Sagua as wantonly and as calmly as a gardener cuts down weeds. The stories of these butcheries were told to me by Englishmen and Americans who could look from their verandas over miles of fields that belonged to them, but who could not venture with safety two hundred yards from their doorsteps.

They were virtually prisoners in their own homes, and every spot of ground within sight of their windows marked where one of their laborers had been cut down, sometimes when he was going to the next *central* on an errand, or to carry the mail, and sometimes when he was digging potatoes or cutting sugarcane within sight of the forts. Passes and orders were of no avail. The guerrillas tore up the passes,

Amateur Surgery in Cuba

and swore later that the men were suspects, and were at the moment of their capture carrying messages to the insurgents. The stories these planters told me were not dragged from them to furnish copy for a newspaper, but came out in the course of our talk, as we walked over the small extent which the forts allowed us.

My host would say, pointing to one of the *pacíficos* huddled in a corner of his machine shop: "That man's brother was killed last week about three hundred yards over there to the left while he was digging in the field." Or, in answer to a question from our consul, he would say: "Oh, that boy who used to take care of your horse—some guerrillas shot him a month ago." After you hear stories like these during an entire day, the air seems to be heavy with murder, and the very ground on which you walk smells of blood. It was the same in the town, where any one was free to visit the *cartel*, and view the murdered bodies of the *pacíficos* hacked and beaten and stretched out as a warning, or for public approbation. There were six so exposed while I was in Sagua. In Matanzas they brought the bodies to the *plaza* at night when the band was playing, and the guerrillas marched around the open place with the bodies of eighteen Cubans swinging from the backs of ponies with their heads hanging down and bumping against the horses' knees. The people flocked to the sides of the *plaza* to applaud this ghastly procession, and the men in the open *cafés* cheered the guerrilla chief and cried, "Long live Spain!"

Speaking dispassionately, and with a full knowledge of the details of many butcheries, it is impossible for me to think of the Spanish guerrillas otherwise than as worse than savage animals. A wild animal kills to obtain food, and not merely for the joy of killing. These guerrillas murder and then laugh over it. The cannibal, who has been supposed hitherto to be the lowest grade of man, is really of a higher caste than these Spanish murderers—men like Colonel Fondevila, Cerreros, and Colonel Bonita—for a cannibal kills to keep himself alive. These men kill to feed their vanity, in order that they may pose as brave soldiers, and that their friends may give them banquets in hotel parlours.

If what I say seems prejudiced and extravagant it may be well to insert this translation from a Spanish paper, *El Pais*:

There are signs of civilization among us; but the truth is that we are uncultured, barbaric and cruel. Although this may not be willingly acknowledged, the fact is that we are committing acts of savagery of which there is no counterpart in any other

Scouring Party of Spanish Cavalry

European country.

Let us not say a word of the atrocities perpetrated at the Castle of Montjuich; of the iniquitous and miserable massacre of the Novelda republicans; of the shootings which occur daily in Manila; of the arbitrary imprisonments which are systematically made here. We wish now to say something of the respect due to the conquered, of generosity that should be shown to prisoners of war, for these are sentiments which exist even among savage people.

The Cuban exiles who disembark at Cadiz are sent on foot to the distant castle of Figueras. 'The unfortunate exiles,' a letter from Carpió says, 'passed here barefooted and bleeding, almost naked and freezing. At every town, far from finding rest for their fatigue, they are received with all sorts of insults; they are scoffed and provoked. I am indignant at this total lack of humanitarian sentiment and charity. I have two sons who are fighting against the Cuban insurgents; but this does not prevent me from denouncing those who ill-treat their prisoners. I have witnessed such outrages upon the unfortunate exiles that I do not hesitate to say that nothing like it has ever occurred in Africa.'

I do not wish what I have said concerning the Florida correspondents to be misunderstood as referring to those who are writing, and have written from the island of Cuba. They suffer from the "*fakirs*" even more than do the people of the United States who read the stories of both, and who confound the sensation-mongers with those who go to find the truth at the risk of their lives. For these latter do risk their lives, daily and hourly, when they go into these conflicts looking for the facts. I have not been in any conflict, so I can speak of these men without fear of being misunderstood.

They are taking chances that no war correspondents ever took in any war in any part of the world. For this is not a war—it is a state of lawless butchery, and the rights of correspondents, of soldiers and of non-combatants are not recognised. Archibald Forbes, and "Bull Run" Russell and Frederick Villiers had great continental armies to protect them; these men work alone with a continental army against them. They risk capture at sea and death by the guns of a Spanish cruiser, and, escaping that, they face when they reach the island the greater danger of capture there and of being cut down by a guerrilla force and left to die in a road, or of being put in a prison and left to die of fever, as Govin was cut down, as Delgardo died in prison, as Melton is lying in prison now, where he will continue to lie until we have a Secretary of State who recognises the rights of the correspondent as a non-combatant, or at least as an American citizen.

The fate of these three American correspondents has not deterred others from crossing the lines and they are in the field now, lying in swamps by day and creeping between the forts by night, standing under fire by the side of Gómez as they stood beside Maceo, going without food, without shelter, without the right to answer the attacks of the Spanish troops, climbing the mountains and crawling across the *trochas*, creeping to some friendly hut for a cup of coffee and to place their despatches in safe hands, and then going back again to run the gauntlet of Spanish spies and of flying columns and of the unspeakable guerrillas.

When you sit comfortably at your breakfast in New York, with a policeman at the corner, and read the despatches which these gentlemen write of Cuban victories and their interviews with self-important Cuban chiefs, you should remember what it cost them to supply you with that addition to your morning's budget of news. Whether the result is worth the risk, or whether it is not paying too great a price, the greatest price of all, for too little, is not the question. The reckless bravery and the unselfishness of the correspondents in the field in Cuba today are beyond parallel.

It is as dangerous to seek for Gómez as Stanley found it to seek for Livingston, and as few men return from the insurgent camps as from the Arctic regions.

In case you do not read a New York paper, it is well that you should know that the names of these correspondents are Grover Flint, Sylvester Scovel and George Bronson Rae. I repeat, that as I could not reach the field, I can write thus freely of those who have been more successful.

The Right of Search of American Vessels

On the boat which carried me from Cuba to Key West were three young girls, who had been exiled for giving aid to the insurgents. The brother of one of them is in command of the Cuban forces in the field near Havana. More than once his sister had joined him there, and had seen fighting and carried back despatches to the *Junta* in Havana. For this she and two other young women, who were also suspected, were ordered to leave the island.

I happened to sit next to this young lady at table on the steamer, and I found that she was not an Amazon nor a Joan of Arc nor a woman of the people, with a machete in one hand and a Cuban flag in the other. She was a well-bred, well-educated young person, speaking three languages.

This is what the Spaniards did to these girls:

After ordering them to leave the island on a certain day they sent detectives to the houses of each on the morning of that day and had them undressed and searched by a female detective to discover if they were carrying letters to the *Junta* at Key West or Tampa. They were searched thoroughly, even to the length of taking off their shoes and stockings. Later, when the young ladies stood at last on the deck of an American vessel, with the American flag hanging from the stern, the Spanish officers followed them there, and demanded that a cabin should be furnished them to which the girls might be taken, and they were then again undressed and searched by this woman for the second time.

For the benefit of people with unruly imaginations, of whom there seem to be a larger proportion in this country than I had supposed, I will state again that the search of these women was conducted by women and not by men, as I was reported to have said, and as I did not say in my original report of the incident.

Spanish officers, with red crosses for bravery on their chests and gold lace on their cuffs, strutted up and down while the search was going on, and chancing to find a Cuban suspect among the passengers, ordered him to be searched also, only they did not give him the privacy of a cabin, but searched his clothes and shoes and hat on the main deck of this American vessel before the other passengers and myself and the ship's captain and his crew.

In order to leave Havana, it is first necessary to give notice of your wish to do so by sending your passport to the captain general, who looks up your record and, after twenty-four hours, if he is willing to let you go, *visés* your passport and so signifies that your request is granted. After you have complied with that requirement of martial law, and the captain general has agreed to let you depart, and you are on board of an American vessel, the Spanish soldiers' control over you and your movements should cease, for they relinquish all their rights when they give you back your passport.

At least the case of Barrundia justifies such a supposition. It was then shown that, while a passenger or a member of a crew is amenable to the "common laws" of the country in the port in which the vessel lies, he is not to be disturbed for political offenses against her government.

When the officers of Guatemala went on board a vessel of the Pacific Mail line and arrested Barrundia, who was a revolutionist, and then shot him between decks, the American minister, who had permitted this outrage, was immediately recalled, and the letter recalling him, which was written by James G. Blaine, clearly and emphatically sets forth the principle that a political offender is not to be molested on board of an American vessel, whether she is in the passenger trade or a ship of war.

Prof. Joseph H. Beale, Jr., the professor of international law at Harvard, said in reference to the case of these women when I first wrote of it:

> So long as a state of war has not been recognised by this country, the Spanish Government has not the right to stop or search our vessels on the high seas for contraband of war or for any other purpose, nor would it have the right to subject American citizens or an American vessel in Cuban waters to treatment which would not be legal in the case of Spanish citizens or vessels.
>
> But the Spanish Government has the right in Cuba to execute

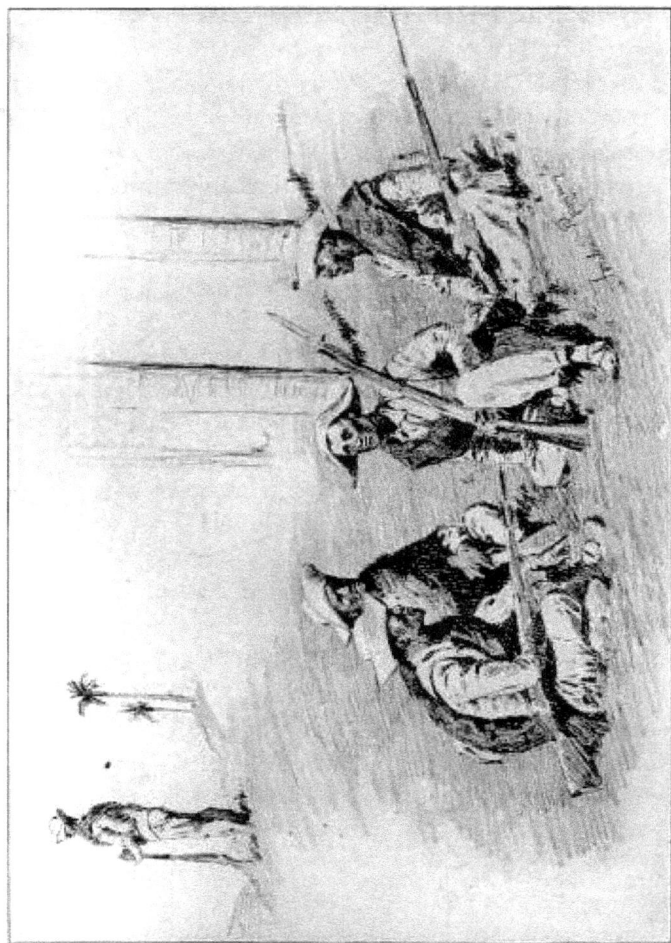

A Spanish Picket Post

upon American citizens or vessels any laws prevailing there, in the same way as they would execute them upon the Spaniards, unless they are prevented by the provisions of some treaty with the United States. The fact that the vessel in the harbour of Havana was flying a neutral flag could not protect it from the execution of Spanish law.

However unwise or inhuman the action of the Spanish authorities may have been in searching the women on board the *Olivette*, they appear to have been within their legal rights.

The Spanish minister at Washington has also declared that his government has the right of search in the harbour of Havana. Hence in the face of two such authorities the question raised is probably answered from a legal point of view. But if that is the law, it would seem well to alter it, for it gives the Spanish authorities absolute control over the persons and property of Americans on American vessels, and that privilege in the hands of persons as unscrupulous and as insolent as are the Spanish detectives, is a dangerous one. So dangerous a privilege, indeed, that there is no reason nor excuse for not keeping an American ship of war in the harbour of Havana.

For suppose that letters and despatches had been found on the persons of these young ladies, and they had been put on shore and lodged in prison; or suppose the whole ship and everyone on board had been searched, as the captain of the *Olivette* said the Spanish officers told him they might decide to do, and letters had been found on the Americans, and they had been ordered over the side and put into prison—would that have been an act derogatory to the dignity of the United States? Or are we to understand that an American citizen or a citizen of any country, after he has asked and obtained permission to leave Cuba and is on board of an American vessel, is no more safe there than he would be in the insurgent camp?

The latter supposition would seem to be correct, and the matter to depend on the captain of the vessel and her owners, from whom he receives his instructions, and not to be one in which the United States government is in any way concerned. I do not believe the captain of a British passenger steamer would have allowed one of his passengers to be searched on the main deck of his vessel, as I saw this Cuban searched; nor even the captain of a British tramp steamer nor of a coal barge.

The chief engineer of the *Olivette* declared to me that in his opinion, "it served them just right," and the captain put a cabin at the disposal of the Spanish spies with eager humility. And when one of the detectives showed some disinclination to give back my passport, and I said I would keep him on board until he did it, the captain said: "Yes, you will, will you? I would like to see you try it," suggesting that he was master of his own ship and of my actions. But he was not. There is not an unwashed, garlicky, bediamonded Spanish spy in Cuba who has not more authority on board the *Olivette* than her American captain and his subservient crew.

Only a year ago half of this country was clamouring for a war with the greatest power it could have selected for that purpose. Yet Great Britain would have been the first to protect her citizens and their property and their self-respect if they had been abused as the self-respect and property and freedom of Americans have been abused by this fourth-rate power, and are being abused today.

Before I went to Cuba I was as much opposed to our interfering there as any other person equally ignorant concerning the situation could be, but since I have seen for myself, I feel ashamed that we should have stood so long idle. We have been too considerate, too fearful that as a younger nation, we should appear to disregard the laws laid down by older nations. We have tolerated what no European power would have tolerated; we have been patient with men who have put back the hand of time for centuries, who lie to our representatives daily, who butcher innocent people, who gamble with the lives of their own soldiers in order to gain a few more stars and an extra stripe, who send American property to the air in flames and murder American prisoners.

The British lately sent an expedition of eight hundred men to the west coast of Africa to punish a savage king who butchers people because it does not rain. Why should we tolerate Spanish savages merely because they call themselves "the most Catholic," but who in reality are no better than this naked negro? What difference is there between the King of Benin who crucifies a woman because he wants rain and General Weyler who outrages a woman for his own pleasure and throws her to his bodyguard of blacks, even if the woman has the misfortune to live after it—and to still live in Sagua la Grande today?

If the English were right—and they were right—in punishing the King of Benin for murdering his subjects to propitiate his idols, we are right to punish these revivers of the Inquisition for starving women and children to propitiate an Austrian archduchess.

It is difficult to know what the American people do want. They

General Weyler in the Field

do not want peace, apparently, for their senators, some through an ignorant hatred of England and others through a personal dislike of the President, emasculated the arbitration treaty; and they do not want war, for, as someone has written, if we did not go to war with Spain when she murdered the crew of the *Virginius* we never will.

But if the executive and the legislators wish to assure themselves, like "Fighting Bob Acres," that they have some right on their side, they need not turn back to the *Virginius* incident. There are reasons enough today to justify their action, if it is to be their intellects and not their feelings that must move them to act. American property has been destroyed by Spanish troops to the amount of many millions, and no answer made to demands of the State Department for an explanation. American citizens have been imprisoned and shot—some without a trial, some in front of their own domiciles, and American vessels are turned over to the uses of the Spanish secret police. These would seem to be sufficient reasons for interfering.

But why should we not go a step farther and a step higher, and interfere in the name of humanity? Not because we are Americans, but because we are human beings, and because, within eighty miles of our coast, Spanish officials are killing men and women as wantonly as though they were field mice, not in battle, but in cold blood—cutting them down in the open roads, at the wells to which they have gone for water, or on their farms, where they have stolen away to dig up a few potatoes, having first run the gauntlets of the forts and risked their lives to obtain them.

This is not an imaginary state of affairs, nor are these supposititious cases. I am writing only of the things I have heard from eye witnesses and of some of the things that I have seen.

President Cleveland declared in his message to Congress:—

When the inability of Spain to deal successfully with the insurgents has become manifest, and it is demonstrated that her sovereignty is extinct in Cuba for all purposes of its rightful existence, and when a hopeless struggle for its re-establishment has degenerated into a strife which is nothing more than the useless sacrifice of human life and the utter destruction of the very subject-matter of the conflict, a situation will be presented in which our obligations to the sovereignty of Spain will be superseded by higher obligations, which we can hardly hesitate to recognise and discharge!

These conditions are now manifest. A hopeless struggle for sovereignty has degenerated into a strife which means not the useless, but the wanton sacrifice of human life, and the utter destruction of the subject-matter of the conflict.

What further manifestations are needed? Is it that the American people doubt the sources from which their information comes? They are the consuls all over the island of Cuba. For what voice crying in the wilderness are they still waiting? What will convince them that the time has come?

If the United States is to interfere in this matter she should do so at once, but she should only do so after she has informed herself thoroughly concerning it. She should not act on the reports of the hotel *piazza* correspondents, but send men to Cuba on whose judgment and common sense she can rely. General Fitzhugh Lee is one of these men, and there is no better informed American on Cuban matters than he, nor one who sees more clearly the course which our government should pursue. Through the consuls all over the island, he is in touch with every part of it, and in daily touch; but incidents which are frightfully true there seem exaggerated and overdrawn when a typewritten description of them reaches the calm corridors of the State Department.

More men like Lee should go to Cuba to inform themselves, not men who will stop in Havana and pick up the gossip of the Hotel Ingleterra, but who will go out into the cities and sugar plantations and talk to the consuls and merchants and planters, both Spanish and American; who can see for themselves the houses burning and the smoke arising from every point of the landscape; who can see the bodies of "*pacificos*" brought into the cities, and who can sit on a porch of an American planter's house and hear him tell in a whisper how his sugarcane was set on fire by the same Spanish soldiers who surround the house, and who are supposed to guard his property, but who, in reality, are there to keep a watch on him.

He should hear little children, born of American parents, come into the consulate and ask for a piece of bread. He should see the children and the women herded in the towns or walking the streets in long processions, with the mayor at their head, begging his fellow Spaniards to give them food, the children covered with the red blotches of smallpox and the women gaunt with yellow fever. He should see hundreds of thousands of dollars' worth of machinery standing idle, covered with rust and dirt, or lying twisted and broken under fallen walls. He will learn that while one hundred and fifty-six vessels came into the port of Matanzas in 1894, only eighty-eight came in 1895, and that but sixteen touched there in 1896, and that while the export of sugar from that port to the United States in 1894 amounted to eleven millions of dollars, in 1895 it sank to eight millions of dollars, and in 1896 it did not reach one million. I copied these figures one morning from the consular books, and that loss of ten millions of dollars in two years in one little port is but a sample of the facts that show what chaos this war is working.

In three weeks, any member of the Senate or of Congress who wishes to inform himself on this reign of terror in Cuba can travel from one end of this island to the other and return competent to speak with absolute authority. No man, no matter what his prejudices may be, can make this journey and not go home convinced that it is his duty to try to stop this cruel waste of life and this wanton destruction of a beautiful country.

A reign of terror sounds hysterical, but it is an exact and truthful descriptive phrase of the condition in Cuba. Insurgents and Spaniards alike are laying waste the land, and neither side shows any sign of giving up the struggle. But while the men are in the field fighting after their fashion, for the independence of the island, the old men and the infirm and the women and children, who cannot help the cause or themselves, and who are destitute and starving and dying, have their eyes turned toward the great republic that lies only eighty miles away, and they are holding out their hands and asking "How long, O, Lord, how long?"

Or if the members of the Senate and of Congress cannot visit Cuba, why will they not listen to those who have been there? Of three men who travelled over the island, seeking the facts concerning it, two correspondents and an interpreter, two of the three were for a time in Spanish hospitals, covered with smallpox. Of the three, although we were together until they were taken ill, I was the only one who escaped contagion.

If these other men should die, they die because they tried to find out the truth. Is it likely, having risked such a price for it that they would lie about what they have seen?

They could have invented stories of famine and disease in Havana. They need not have looked for the facts where they were to be found, in the seaports and villages and fever camps. Why not listen to these men or to Stephen Bonsai, of the *New York Herald*, in whom the late

President showed his confidence by appointing him to two diplomatic missions?

Why not listen to C.E. Akers, of the *London Times*, and *Harper's Weekly*, who has held two commissions from the queen? Why disregard a dozen other correspondents who are seeking the truth, and who urge in every letter which they write that their country should stop this destruction of a beautiful land and this butchery of harmless non-combatants?

The matter lies at the door of Congress. Each day's delay means the death of hundreds of people, every hour sees fresh blood spilled, and more houses and more acres of crops sinking into ashes. A month's delay means the loss to this world of thousands of lives, the unchecked growth of terrible diseases, and the spreading devastation of a great plague.

It would be an insult to urge political reasons, or the sure approval of the American people which the act of interference would bring, or any other unworthy motive. No European power dare interfere, and it lies with the United States and with her people to give the signal. If it is given now it will save thousands of innocent lives; if it is delayed just that many people will perish.

For Cuba Libre

Letters From Cuba

In December, 1896, Richard and Frederic Remington, the artist, were commissioned by the New York *Journal* to visit Cuba which was then at war with Spain. It was their intention to go from Key West in the *Vamoose*, a very fast but frail steam-launch, and to make a landing at some uninhabited point on the Cuban coast. After this their plans seem to have been to trust to luck and the kindliness of the revolutionists. After waiting for some time at Key West for favourable weather, they at last started out on a dark night to make the crossing. A few hours after the *Vamoose* had left Key West a heavy storm arose—apparently much too violent for the slightly built launch.

The crew struck and the captain finally refused to go on to Cuba and put back to Key West. Shortly after this Remington and my brother reached Havana by a more simple and ostentatious route. This was my brother's first effort as a war correspondent, and I presume it was this fact and the very indefiniteness of the original plan that caused his mother and father so much uneasiness. And, indeed, it did prove eventually a hazardous exploit.

On way to Key West.
December 19, 1896.

Dear Mother:

I hope you won't be cross with me for going off and not letting you know, but I thought it was better to do it that way as there was such delay in our getting started. I am going to Cuba by way of Key West with Frederic Remington and Michaelson, a correspondent who has been there for six months. We are to be taken by the *Vamoose* the fastest steam yacht made to Santa Clara province where the Cubans will meet us and take us to Gomez. We will stay a month with him, the yacht calling for copy and sketches once a week, and finally for us in a month. I get all my expenses and *The Journal* pays me

$3,000 for the month's work. The *Harper's Magazine* also takes a story at six hundred dollars and Russell will reprint Remington's sketches and my story in book form, so I shall probably clear $4,000 in the next month or six weeks.

I was a week in getting information on the subject so I know all about it from the men who have just been there and I want you to pay attention to what I tell you they told me and not to listen to any stray visitor who comes in for tea and talks without any tact or knowledge. There is no danger in the trip except the problem of getting there and getting away again, and that is now removed by *The Journal's* yacht. I would have gone earlier had any of the periodicals that asked me to go shown me any way to get there—*There is no fever this time of year* and as you know fever never touches me. It got all the others in Central America and never worried me at all. There is no danger of getting shot, as the province into which we go, the Santa Clara province, is owned and populated and patrolled by the Cubans. It is no more Spanish than New Jersey and the Spaniards cannot get in there.

We have the strongest possible letters from the *Junta*, and I have from Lamont, Bayard and Olney and credentials in every language. We will sit around the Gomez camp and send messengers back to the coast. It is a three days trip and as Gomez may be moving from place to place you may not hear from us for a month and we may not hear from you but remember it was a much longer time than that before you heard from me when I went to Honduras. Also keep in mind that I am going as a correspondent only and must keep out of the way of fighting and that I mean to do so, as Chamberlain says we want descriptive stories not brave deeds—Major Flint who has arranged the trip for us was down there with Maceo as a correspondent.

He saw six fights and never shot off his gun once because as he said it was not his business to kill people and he has persuaded me that he is right, so I won't do anything but look on—I have bought at *The Journal's* expense a fifty dollar field glass which is a new invention and the best made. I have marked it so that you can see a man five miles off and as soon as I see him I mean to begin to ride or run the other way—no one loves himself more than I do so you leave me to take care of myself.

I wish I could give you any idea of the contempt the four returned correspondents who talked to me, have for the Spaniards. They have seen them shoot 2,500 rounds without hitting men at 200 yards and they run away if the enemy begins on them first.

However, you trust to Richard—We have a fine escort arranged for us and Michaelson speaks Spanish perfectly and has been six months scouting over the country.   Dick.

Dear Family:

I got your letters late last night and they made me pretty solemn. It is an awfully solemn thing to have people care for you like that and to care for them as I do. I can't tell you how much I love you. You don't know how much the pain of worrying you for a month has meant to me, but I have talked it all out with myself, and left it to God and I am sure I am doing right. As Mrs. Crown said, "There's a whole churchful up here praying for you," and I guess that will pull me through. Of course, dear, dear Mother thought she was cross with me. She could not be cross with me, and her letter told me how much she cared, that was all, and made me be extra careful. But I need not promise you to be careful. You have an idea I am a wild, filibustering, hot-headed young man. I am not. I gave the guides to understand their duty was to keep us out of danger if we had to walk miles to avoid it.

We are men of peace, going in, as real estate agents and coffee-planters and drummers are going in on every steamer, to attend to our especial work and get out again quick. I have just as strong a prejudice against killing a man as I have against his killing me. Lots and lots of love. Don't get scared if you don't hear for a month, although we will try to get our stories back once a week, but you know we are at the convenience of the Cubans who will pocket our despatches and money and not take the long trip back. Thank dear Dad for his letter full of good advice. It was excellent. Remington and Michelson are good men and I like them immensely. Already we are firm friends.

Love,   Dick.

Key West—January 1, 1897.

Dear Mother:

As you will know by my telegram, we are either off on a safe sea going boat or waiting for one. There is no turning back from here and the only reason I thought of doing so was the knowledge of the way you would suffer and worry. I argued it out that it was selfish in me to weigh my getting laughed at and paragraphed as the war correspond-ent that always Turned Back against a month of uneasiness for you, but later I saw I could not do it much as I love you for the element of danger to me is non-existent; it is merely an exciting adventure and you will have to believe me and not worry but be a Spartan mother.

I would not count being laughed at and the loss of my own self-respect if I really thought there was great danger, but I do not. You will not lose me and if I go now, I can sit still next time and say "I have done better things than that." If I had not gone it would have meant that I would have had to have done just that much harder a stunt next time to make people forget that I had failed in this one. Now do cheer up and believe in the luck of Richard Harding Davis and the British Army. We have *carte blanche* from *The Journal* to buy or lease any boat on the coast and I rocked them for $1000 in advance payment because of the delay over the *Vamoose*.

I am so happy at thinking I am going, I could not have faced any-one had I not, although we had nothing to do with the failure, we tried to cross fairly in the damn tub and it was her captain who put back. I lay out on the deck and cried when he refused to go ahead, we had waited so long. The Cubans and Remington and Michelson had put on all their riding things but fortunately I had not and so was spared that humiliation.

What I don't know about the Fine Art of Filibustering now is unnecessary. I find many friends of my Captain Boynton or "Capt. Burke." Tonight, the officers of the *Raleigh* give me a grand dinner at which I wear a dress suit and make speeches—they are the best chaps I ever met in the navy, Lots of love and best wishes to Dad and to Nora for a happy, happy New Year. You know me and you know my con-science but it would not let me go back in order to save you anxiety so you won't think me selfish. God bless you.

Dick

Key West, January 2nd, 1897.

Dear Family:

I have learned here that the first quality needed to make a great filibuster is Patience, it is not courage, or resources or a knowledge of the Cuban Coast line, it is patience. Anybody can run a boat into a dark bayou and dump rifles on the beach and scurry away to sea again but only heroes can sit for a month on a hotel porch or at the end of a wharf, and wait. That is all we do and that is my life at Key West. I get up and half dress and take a plunge in the bay and then dress fully and have a greasy breakfast and then light a huge Key West cigar, price three cents and sit on the hotel porch with my feet on a rail—Noth-ing happens after that except getting one's boots polished as the two industries of this place are blacking boots and driving cabs.

I have two boys to black mine at the same time every morning and pay the one who does his the better of the two—It generally ends in a fight so that affords diversion—Then a man comes along, any man, and says, "Remington's looking for you" and I get up and look for Remington. There is only a triangle of streets where one can find him and I call at "Josh" Curry's first and then at Pendleton's News Store and read all the back numbers of the *Police Gazette* for the hundredth time and then call here at the Custom House and then look in at the Cable office, where Michaelson lives sending telegrams about anything or nothing and that brings me back to the hotel porch again, where I have my boots shined once more and then go into mid-day dinner.

In the meanwhile, Remington is looking for me a hundred yards in the rear. He generally gets to "Josh's" as I leave the Custom House— In the afternoon I study Spanish out of a text book and at three take a bicycle ride, at five I call at the garrison to take tea with the doctor and his wife, who is sweeter than angel's ever get to be with a minia- ture angel of a baby called Martha. I wait until retreat is sounded and the gun is fired at sunset and having commented unfavourably on the way the soldiers let the flag drop on the grass instead of catching it on the arms as a bluejacket does, I ride off to the bay for another bath—Then I take the launch to the *Raleigh* and dine with the of- ficers and rejoice in the clean fresh paint and brass and decks and the lights and black places of a great ship of war, than which nothing is more splendid.

We sit on the quarter-deck and smoke and play the guitar and I go home again, in time for bed. I vary this programme occasionally by spending the morning on the end of a wharf watching another man fish and reading old novels and the *Lives of Captain Walker* and *Captain Fry of the Virginius*, two great books from each of which I am going to write a short story like the one of the Alamo or of the Jameson Raid—The life of Walker I found on the *Raleigh* and the life of Cap- tain Fry with all the old wood cuts and the newspaper comments of the time at a book store here.

I don't know when we shall get away but it is no use kicking about it, Michaelson is doing all he can and the new tug will be along in a week anyway. I shall be so glad to get to Cuba that I will dance with glee.

Dick.

Dear Mother:

I sent you a note by Remington which he will mail in the States—From here I go to Sagua La Grande. It is on the northern coast. I think from there I shall cross over to Cienfuegos on the Southern coast and then if I can catch a steamer go to Santiago to see my old friends, at the Juraqua mines and MacWilliams' ore road and "the Palms"—Everywhere I am treated well on account of Weyler's order and I am learning a great deal and talking very little, my Spanish being bad. There is war here and no mistake and all the people in the fields have been ordered in to the fortified towns where they are starving and dying of disease.

Yesterday I saw the houses of these people burning on both sides of the track—They gave shelter to the insurgents and so very soon they found their houses gone. I am so relieved at getting old Remington to go as though I had won $5000. He was a splendid fellow but a perfect kid and had to be humoured and petted all the time. I shall if I have luck be through with this in a few weeks but it has had such a set back at the start that I am afraid it can never make a book and I doubt if I can write a decent article even. I am so anxious not to keep you worrying any longer than is necessary and so I am hurrying along taking only a car window view of things.

Address me care of Consul General Lee, Havana and confine your remarks to what is going on at home. I know what is going on here. I don't believe half I hear but I am being slowly converted. Remington is more excitable than I am, so don't misunderstand if he starts in violently. I am getting details and verifying things. He is right on a big scale but everyone has lied so about this island that I do not want to say anything I do not believe is true. This is a beautiful little city and after Jaruco, where we slept two days ago, it is Paris. There we slept off the barnyard and cows and chickens walked all over the floor and fleas all over us. It was like Honduras only filthier. Speaking of Paris, tell the Kid I expect to go over to him soon after I return to New York.

Lots of love.

Dick.

Cardenas—North Coast of Cuba.
January 16th, 1897.

Dear Mother:

It is very funny not knowing what sort of a place you are to sleep in next and taking things out of a grab bag, as it were—In Europe you can always guess what the well-known towns will give you for you have a guide book, but here it is all luck. Matanzas was a pretty city but the people were awful, the hotel was Spanish and the proprietor insolent, though I was spending more of Willie Hearst's money than all of the officers spend in a week, the consul could not talk English or Spanish, he said he hadn't come there "to go to school to no Spaniard" and he gloried in the fact he had been there three years without knowing a word of the language. His vice-consul was worse and everything went wrong generally.

Everyone I met was an alarmist and that is polite for liar. They asked Remington if he was the man who manufactured the rifles and gave us the *Iowa Democrat* to read. Tonight I reached here after a six hours ride through blazing fields of sugarcane and stopped on my way to the hotel to ask the consul when the next boat went to Sagua la Grande—I had no letter of introduction to him as I had to the Matanzas consul, but as soon as he saw my card he got out of his chair and shook hands again and was as hearty and well-bred and delightful as Charley himself and unlike Chas he did not ask me 14 *francs* for looking on him. He is out now chasing around to get me a train for tomorrow. But I won't go tomorrow.

My hotel looks on the *plaza* and the proprietor and the whole suite of attendants are my slaves. It is just as different as can be. My interpreter does it, he calls himself my valet, although I point out to him that two shirts and twelve collars do not constitute a wardrobe even with a rubber coat thrown in. But he likes to play at my being a distinguished stranger and I can't say I object. Only when you remember the way I was invited to see Cuba and expected to see it, and now the way I am seeing it from car windows with a *valet*. What would the new school of yellow kid journalists say if they knew that.

For the first time on this trip I have wished you were both with me, that was to night. I never see anything really beautiful but that it instantly makes me feel selfish and wish you could see it too. It has happened again and again and tonight I wish you could be here with me on this balcony. The town runs down a slope to the bay and in the middle of it is the *plaza* with me on the balcony which lets out of my sleeping room—"the room" so the proprietor tells me, "reserved only for the *Capitain General*."

It is just like the description in that remarkable novel of mine where Clay and Alice sit on the balcony of the restaurant. I have the moonlight and the cathedral with the open doors and the bronze statue in the middle and the royal palms moving in the breeze straight from the sea and the people walking around the *plaza* below. If it was in any way as beautiful as this Clay and Alice would have ended the novel that night.

I got a grand lot of letters today which Otto, my interpreter brought back from Havana after having conducted Remington there in safety. I must say you are writing very cheerfully now, but I don't wonder you worried at first but now that I am a commercial traveller with an order from Weyler which does everything when I find it necessary, you really must not worry any more but just let me continue on my uneventful journey and then come home. I shall have been gone so long and my friends, judging from Russell and Dana and Irene's letters, will be so glad to see me, that they will have forgotten I went out to do other things than coast around in trains.

As a matter of fact this is a terribly big problem and most difficult to get the truth of, I find myself growing to be the opposite of the alarmist, whatever that is, although you would think the picturesque and dramatic and exciting thing would be the one I would rather believe because I want to believe it, but I find that that is not so, I see a great deal on both sides and I do not believe half I am told.

As we used to say at collie, "it is against history," and it is against history for men to act as I am told they are acting here—They show me the *pueblo* huddled together around the fortified towns, living in palm huts but I know that they have always lived in palm huts, the yellow kid reporters don't know that or consider it, but send off word that the condition of the people is terrible, that they have only leaves to cover them, and it sounds very badly. That is an instance of what I mean. In a big way there is no doubt that the process going on here is one of extermination and ruin. Two years ago, the amount of sugar shipped from the port of Matanzas to the U. S. was valued at 11 millions a year. This last year just over shows that sugar to the amount of $800,000 was sent out. In '94, 154 vessels touched at Matanzas on their way to America. In '95 there were 80 and in '96 there are 16.

I always imagined that houses were destroyed during a war because they got in the way of cannon balls or they were burned because they might offer shelter to the enemy, but here they are destroyed, with the purpose of making the war horrible and hurrying up the end. The insurgents began first by destroying the sugar mills, some of which were worth millions of dollars in machinery, and now the Spaniards are burning the homes of the people and herding them in around the towns to starve out the insurgents and to leave them without shelter or places to go for food or to hide the wounded.

So, all day long where ever you look you see great heavy columns of smoke rising into this beautiful sky above the magnificent palms the most noble of all palms, almost of all trees—It is the most beautiful country I have ever visited. I had no recollection of how beautiful it was or else I had not the knowledge of other places with which to compare it. Nothing out of the imagination can approach it in its great waterfalls and mossy rocks and grand plains and forests of white pillars with plumes waving above them.

Only man is vile here and it is cruel to see the walls of the houses with blind eyes, with roofs gone and gardens burned, every church but one that I have seen was a fortress with hammocks swung from the altars and rude barricades thrown up around the doorways—If this is war I am of the opinion that it is a senseless wicked institution made for soldiers, lovers and correspondents for different reasons, and for no one else in the world and it is too expensive for the others to keep it going to entertain these few gentlemen—I have seen very little of it yet and I probably won't see much more, but I have seen all I want.

Remington had his mind satisfied even sooner—but then he is an alarmist and exaggerates things—The men who wear the red badge of courage, I don't feel sorry for, they have their reward in their bloody bandages and the little cross on their tunic but those you meet coming back sick and dying with fever are the ones that make fighting contemptible—poor little farmers, poor little children with no interest in Cuba or Spain's right to hold it, who have been sent out to die like ants before they have learned to hold a Mauser, and who are going back again with the beards that have grown in the field hospitals on their cheeks and their eyes hollow, and too weak to move or speak.

Six of them died while I was in Jaroco, a town as big as Marion and that had been the average for two months, think of that, six people dying in Marion every day through July and August—I didn't stay in that town any longer than the train did—Well I have been writing editorials here instead of cheering you up but I guess I'm about right and when I see a little more I'll tell it over again to *The Journal*—It is not as exciting reading as deeds of daring by our special correspondent and I haven't changed my name or shaved my eyebrows or done anything the other men have done but I believe I am getting near the truth.

They have shut off provisions going or coming from the towns, they have huddled hundreds of people who do not know what a bath means around these towns, and this is going to happen—As soon as the rains begin the yellow fever and smallpox will set in and all vessels leaving Cuban ports will be quarantined and the island will be one great plague spot. The insurgents who are in the open fields will live and the soldiers will die for their officers know nothing of sanitation or care nothing.

The little consul has just been here to see me and we have had a long talk and I got back at him. He told me he had seen the Franco-German war as a correspondent of *The Tribune* and I asked him if he had ever met another correspondent of *The Tribune* at that time a German student named Hans who cabled the story of the Battle of Gravellote and who Archibald Forbes says was the first correspondent to use the cable.

The consul who looks like William D. Howells wriggled around in his chair and said "I guess you mean me but I was not a German student, I was born and raised in Philadelphia and Forbes got my name wrong, it is Hance."

So, then I got up and shook hands with him in my turn and told him I had always wanted to meet that correspondent and did not expect to do so in Cardenas, on the coast of Cuba.

Thank you all for your letters. I am glad you liked the Jameson book. I thought you knew I was a F. R. G. S. It was George Curzon proposed me and as he is a gold medallist of the Society it was easy getting in.

Lots of love.

Dick

★★★★★★

Richard returned to New York from Cuba in February, 1897, but the following month started for Florence to pay me a long-promised visit. On his way he stopped for a few days in London and Paris.

The Rough Riders at Guasimas

On the day the American troops landed on the coast of Cuba, the Cubans informed General Wheeler that the enemy were intrenched at Guasimas, blocking the way to Santiago. Guasimas is not a village, nor even a collection of houses; it is the meeting place of two trails which join at the apex of a V, three miles from the seaport town of Siboney, and continue merged in a single trail to Santiago. General Wheeler, guided by the Cubans, reconnoitred this trail on the 23rd of June, and with the position of the enemy fully explained to him, returned to Siboney and informed General Young and Colonel Wood that on the following morning he would attack the Spanish position at Guasimas. It has been stated that at Guasimas, the Rough Riders were trapped in an ambush, but, as the plan was discussed while I was present, I know that so far from anyones running into an ambush, every one of the officers concerned had a full knowledge of where he would find the enemy, and what he was to do when he found him.

That night no one slept, for until two o'clock in the morning, troops were still being disembarked in the surf, and two ships of war had their searchlights turned on the landing-place, and made Siboney as light as a ballroom. Back of the searchlights was an ocean white with moonlight, and on the shore red campfires, at which the half-drowned troops were drying their uniforms, and the Rough Riders, who had just marched in from Baiquiri, were cooking a late supper, or early breakfast of coffee and bacon.

Below the former home of the Spanish *comandante*, which General Wheeler had made his headquarters, lay the camp of the Rough Riders, and through it, Cuban officers were riding their half-starved ponies, and scattering the ashes of the campfires. Below them was the beach and the roaring surf, in which a thousand or so naked men were assisting and impeding the progress shoreward of their comrades, in pontoons and shore boats, which were being hurled at the beach like sleds down a water chute.

It was one of the most weird and remarkable scenes of the war, probably of any war. An army was being landed on an enemy's coast at the dead of night, but with the same cheers and shrieks and laughter that rise from the bathers at Coney Island on a hot Sunday. It was a pandemonium of noises. The men still to be landed from the "prison hulks," as they called the transports, were singing in chorus, the men already on shore were dancing naked around the campfires on the beach, or shouting with delight as they plunged into the first bath that had offered in seven days, and those in the launches as they were pitched headfirst at the soil of Cuba, signalised their arrival by howls of triumph. On either side rose black overhanging ridges, in the lowland between were white tents and burning fires, and from the ocean came the blazing, dazzling eyes of the searchlights shaming the quiet moonlight.

After three hours' troubled sleep in this tumult the Rough Riders left camp at five in the morning. With the exception of half a dozen officers they were dismounted, and carried their blanket rolls, haversacks, ammunition, and carbines. General Young had already started toward Guasimas the First and Tenth dismounted cavalry, and according to the agreement of the night before had taken the eastern trail to our right, while the Rough Riders climbed the steep ridge above Siboney and started toward the rendezvous along the trail to the west, which was on high ground and a half mile to a mile distant from the trail along which General Young and his regulars were marching. There was a valley between us, and the bushes were so thick on both sides of our trail that it was not possible at any time, until we met at Guasimas, to distinguish the other column.

As soon as the Rough Riders had reached the top of the ridge, not twenty minutes after they had left camp, which was the first opportunity that presented itself, Colonel Wood ordered Captain Capron to proceed with his troop in front of the column as an advance guard, and to choose a "point" of five men skilled as scouts and trailers. Still in advance of these he placed two Cuban scouts. The column then continued along the trail in single file. The Cubans were at a distance of two hundred and fifty yards; the "point" of five picked men under Sergeant Byrne and Duty-Sergeant Fish followed them at a distance of a hundred yards, and then came Capron's troop of sixty men strung out in single file. No flankers were placed for the reason that the dense undergrowth and the tangle of vines that stretched from the branches of the trees to the bushes below made it a physical impossibility for man or beast to move forward except along the single trail.

Colonel Wood rode at the head of the column, followed by two regular army officers who were members of General Wheeler's staff, a Cuban officer, and Lieutenant-Colonel Roosevelt. They rode slowly in consideration of the troopers on foot, who under a cruelly hot sun carried heavy burdens. To those who did not have to walk, it was not unlike a hunting excursion in our West; the scenery was beautiful and the view down the valley one of luxuriant peace. Roosevelt had never been in the tropics and Captain McCormick and I were talking back at him over our shoulders and at each other, pointing out unfamiliar trees and birds.

Roosevelt thought it looked like a good deer country, as it once was; it reminded McCormick of Southern California; it looked to me like the trails in Central America. We advanced, talking in that fashion and in high spirits, and congratulating ourselves in being shut of the transport and on breathing fine mountain air again, and on the fact that we were on horseback. We agreed it was impossible to appreciate that we were really at war—that we were in the enemy's country. We had been riding in this pleasant fashion for an hour and a half with brief halts for rest, when Wood stopped the head of the column, and rode down the trail to meet Capron, who was coming back. Wood returned immediately, leading his horse, and said to Roosevelt:

Pass the word back to keep silence in the ranks.

The place at which we had halted was where the trail narrowed, and proceeded sharply downward. There was on one side of it a stout barbed-wire fence of five strands. By some fortunate accident this fence had been cut just where the head of the column halted. On the left of the trail it shut off fields of high grass blocked at every fifty yards with great barricades of undergrowth and tangled trees and *chapparal*. On the other side of the trail there was not a foot of free ground; the bushes seemed absolutely impenetrable, as indeed they were later found to be.

When we halted, the men sat down beside the trail and chewed the long blades of grass, or fanned the air with their hats. They had no knowledge of the situation such as their leaders possessed, and their only emotion was one of satisfaction at the chance the halt gave them to rest and to shift their packs. Wood again walked down the trail with Capron and disappeared, and one of the officers informed us that the scouts had seen the outposts of the enemy. It did not seem reasonable that the Spaniards, who had failed to attack us when we landed at Baiquiri, would oppose us until they could do so in force, so, personally, I doubted that there were any Spaniards nearer than Santiago. But we tied our horses to the wire fence, and Capron's troop knelt with carbines at the "Ready," peering into the bushes.

We must have waited there, while Wood reconnoitred, for over ten minutes. Then he returned, and began deploying his troops out at either side of the trail. Capron, he sent on down the trail itself. G Troop was ordered to beat into the bushes on the right, and K and A were sent over the ridge on which we stood down into the hollow to connect with General Young's column on the opposite side of the valley. F and E Troops were deployed in skirmish-line on the other side of the wire fence. Wood had discovered the enemy a few hundred yards from where he expected to find him, and so far from being "surprised," he had time, as I have just described, to get five of his troops into position before a shot was fired. The firing, when it came, started suddenly on our right. It sounded so close that—still believing we were acting on a false alarm, and that there were no Spaniards ahead of us—I guessed it was Capron's men firing at random to disclose the enemy's position.

I ran after G Troop under Captain Llewellyn, and found them breaking their way through the bushes in the direction from which the volleys came. It was like forcing the walls of a maze. If each trooper had not kept in touch with the man on either hand he would have been lost in the thicket. At one moment the underbrush seemed swarming with our men, and the next, except that you heard the twigs breaking, and heavy breathing or a crash as a vine pulled someone down, there was not a sign of a human being anywhere. In a few minutes we broke through into a little open place in front of a dark curtain of vines, and the men fell on one knee and began returning the fire that came from it.

The enemy's fire was exceedingly heavy, and his aim was excellent. We saw nothing of the Spaniards, except a few on the ridge across the valley. I happened to be the only one present with field glasses, and when I discovered this force on the ridge, and had made sure, by the cockades in their *sombreros*, that they were Spaniards and not Cubans, I showed them to Roosevelt. He calculated they were five hundred yards from us, and ordered the men to fire on them at that range. Through the two hours of fighting that followed, although men were falling all around us, the Spaniards on the ridge were the only ones that many of us saw. But the fire against us was not more than eighty yards away, and so hot that our men could only lie flat in the grass and return it in that position.

It was at this moment that our men believed they were being attacked by Capron's troop, which they imagined must have swung to the right, and having lost its bearings and hearing them advancing through the underbrush, had mistaken them for the enemy. They accordingly ceased firing and began shouting in order to warn Capron that he was shooting at his friends. This is the foundation for the statement that the Rough Riders had fired on each other, which they did not do then or at any other time. Later we examined the relative position of the trail which Capron held, and the position of G Troop, and they were at right angles to one another.

Capron could not possibly have fired into us at any time, unless he had turned directly around in his tracks and aimed up the very trail he had just descended. Advancing, he could no more have hit us than he could have seen us out of the back of his head. When we found many hundred spent cartridges of the Spaniards a hundred yards in front of G Troop's position, the question as to who had fired on us was answered.

It was an exceedingly hot corner. The whole troop was gathered in the little open place blocked by the network of grape-vines and tangled bushes before it. They could not see twenty feet on three sides of them, but on the right hand lay the valley, and across it came the sound of Young's brigade, who were apparently heavily engaged. The enemy's fire was so close that the men could not hear the word of command, and Captain Llewellyn and Lieutenant Greenway, unable to get their attention, ran among them, batting them with their *sombreros* to make them cease firing. Lieutenant-Colonel Roosevelt ran up just then, bringing with him Lieutenant Woodbury Kane and ten troopers from K Troop. Roosevelt lay down in the grass beside Llewellyn and consulted with him eagerly. Kane was smiling with the charming content of a perfectly happy man.

When Captain Llewellyn told him his men were not needed, and to rejoin his troop, he led his detail over the edge of the hill on which we lay. As he disappeared below the crest, he did not stoop to avoid the bullets, but walked erect, still smiling. Roosevelt pointed out that it was impossible to advance farther on account of the network of wild grape-vines that masked the Spaniards from us, and that we must cross the trail and make to the left. The shouts the men had raised to warn

Capron had established our position to the enemy, and the firing was now fearfully accurate. Sergeant Russell, who in his day had been a colonel on a governor's staff, was killed, and the other sergeant was shot through the wrist. In the space of three minutes nine men were lying on their backs helpless.

Before we got away, every third man was killed, or wounded. We drew off slowly to the left, dragging the wounded with us. Owing to the low aim of the enemy, we were forced to move on our knees and crawl. Even then men were hit. One man near me was shot through the head. Returning later to locate the body and identify him, I found that the buzzards had torn off his lips and his eyes. This mutilation by these hideous birds was, without doubt, what Admiral Sampson mistook for the work of the Spaniards, when the bodies of the marines at Guantanamo were found disfigured. K Troop meantime had deployed into the valley under the fire from the enemy on the ridge.

It had been ordered to establish communication with General Young's column, and while advancing and firing on the ridge, Captain Jenkins sent the guidon bearer back to climb the hill and wave his red and white banner where Young's men could see it. The guidon bearer had once run for Congress on the gold ticket in Arizona, and, as someone said, was naturally the man who should have been selected for a forlorn hope. His flag brought him instantly under a heavy fire, but he continued waving it until the Tenth Cavalry on the other side of the valley answered, and the two columns were connected by a skirmish-line composed of K Troop and A, under Captain "Bucky" O'Neill.

G Troop meanwhile had hurried over to the left, and passing through the opening in the wire fence had spread out into open order. It followed down after Captain Luna's troop and D and E Troops, which were well already in advance. Roosevelt ran forward and took command of the extreme left of this line. Wood was walking up and down along it, leading his horse, which he thought might be of use in case he had to move quickly to alter his original formation. His plan, at present, was to spread out his men so that they would join Young on the right, and on the left swing around until they flanked the enemy. K and A Troops had already succeeded in joining hands with Young's column across the valley, and as they were capable of taking care of themselves, Wood was bending his efforts to keep his remaining four companies in a straight line and revolving them around the enemy's "end."

It was in no way an easy thing to do. The men were at times wholly hidden from each other, and from him; probably at no one time did he see more than two of his troops together. It was only by the firing that he could tell where his men lay, and that they were always advancing.

The advances were made in quick, desperate rushes—sometimes the ground gained was no more than a man covers in sliding for a base.

At other times half a troop would rise and race forward and then burrow deep in the hot grass and fire. On this side of the line there was an occasional glimpse of the enemy. But for a great part of the time the men shot at the places from where the enemy's fire seemed to come, aiming low and answering in steady volleys. The fire discipline was excellent. The prophets of evil of the Tampa Bay Hotel had foretold that the cowboys would shoot as they chose, and, in the field, would act independently of their officers. As it turned out, the cowboys were the very men who waited most patiently for the officers to give the word of command. At all times the movement was without rest, breathless and fierce, like a cane-rush, or a street fight. After the first three minutes every man had stripped as though for a wrestling match, throwing off all his impedimenta but his cartridge-belt and canteen. Even then the sun handicapped their strength cruelly. The enemy was hidden in the shade of the jungle, while they, for every thicket they gained, had to fight in the open, crawling through grass which was as hot as a steam bath, and with their flesh and clothing torn by thorns and the sword-like blade of the Spanish "bayonet." The glare of the sun was full in their eyes and as fierce as a lime-light.

When G Troop passed on across the trail to the left I stopped at the place where the column had first halted—it had been converted into a dressing station and the wounded of G Troop were left there in the care of the hospital stewards. A tall, gaunt young man with a cross on his arm was just coming back up the trail. His head was bent, and by some surgeon's trick he was carrying a wounded man much heavier than himself across his shoulders. As I stepped out of the trail, he raised his head, and smiled and nodded, and left me wondering where I had seen him before, smiling in the same cheery, confident way and moving in that same position. I knew it could not have been under the same conditions, and yet he was certainly associated with another time of excitement and rush and heat.

Then I remembered him. As now he had been covered with blood and dirt and perspiration, but then he wore a canvas jacket and the man he carried on his shoulders was trying to hold him back from a white-washed line. And I recognised the young doctor, with the blood bathing his breeches, as "Bob" Church, of Princeton.

That was only one of four badly wounded men he carried that day on his shoulders over a half-mile of trail that stretched from the firing-line back to the dressing station and under an unceasing fire. (For this "distinguished gallantry in action," James R. Church later received the medal of honour.) As the senior surgeon was absent he had chief responsibility that day for all the wounded, and that so few of them died is greatly due to this young man who went down into the firing-line and pulled them from it, and bore them out of danger. The comic paragraphers who wrote of the members of the Knickerbocker Club and the college swells of the Rough Riders and of their imaginary valets and golf clubs, should, in decency, since the fight at Guasimas apologize. For the same spirit that once sent these men down a white-washed field against their opponents' rush line was the spirit that sent Church, Channing, Devereux, Ronalds, Wrenn, Cash, Bull, Lamed, Goodrich, Greenway, Dudley Dean, and a dozen others through the high hot grass at Guasimas, not shouting, as their friends the cowboys did, but each with his mouth tightly shut, with his eyes on the ball, and moving in obedience to the captain's signals.

Judging from the sound, our firing-line now seemed to be half a mile in advance of the place where the head of the column had first halted. This showed that the Spaniards had been driven back at least three hundred yards from their original position. It was impossible to see any of our men in the field, so I ran down the trail with the idea that it would lead me back to the troop I had left when I had stopped at the dressing station. The walk down that trail presented one of the most grewsome pictures of the war. It narrowed as it descended; it was for that reason the enemy had selected that part of it for the attack, and the vines and bushes interlaced so closely above it that the sun could not come through.

The rocks on either side were spattered with blood and the rank grass was matted with it. Blanket rolls, haversacks, carbines, and canteens had been abandoned all along its length. It looked as though a retreating army had fled along it, rather than that one troop had fought its way through it to the front. Except for the clatter of the land-crabs, those hideous orchid-coloured monsters that haunt the places of the dead, and the whistling of the bullets in the trees, the place was as silent as a grave. For the wounded lying along its length were as still as the dead beside them. The noise of the loose stones rolling under my feet brought a hospital steward out of the brush, and he called after me:

"Lieutenant Thomas is badly wounded in here, and we can't move him. We want to carry him out of the sun some place, where there is shade and a breeze." Thomas was the first lieutenant of Capron's troop. He is a young man, large and powerfully built. He was shot through the leg just below the trunk, and I found him lying on a blanket half naked and covered with blood, and with his leg bound in tourniquets made of twigs and pocket-handkerchiefs. It gave one a thrill of awe and wonder to see how these cowboy surgeons, with a stick that one would use to light a pipe and with the gaudy 'kerchiefs they had taken from their necks, were holding death at bay. The young officer was in great pain and tossing and raving wildly.

When we gathered up the corners of his blanket and lifted him, he tried to sit upright, and cried out, "You're taking me to the front, aren't you? You said you would. They've killed my captain—do you understand? They've killed Captain Capron. The —— Mexicans! They've killed my captain."

The troopers assured him they were carrying him to the firing-line, but he was not satisfied. We stumbled over the stones and vines, bumping his wounded body against the ground and leaving a black streak in the grass behind us, but it seemed to hurt us more than it did him, for he sat up again clutching at us imploringly with his bloody hands.

"For God's sake, take me to the front," he begged. "Do you hear? I order you; damn you, I order—We must give them hell; do you hear? we must give them hell. They've killed Capron. They've killed my captain."

The loss of blood at last mercifully silenced him, and when we had reached the trail he had fainted and I left them kneeling around him, their grave boyish faces filled with sympathy and concern.

Only fifty feet from him and farther down the trail I passed his captain, with his body propped against Church's knee and with his head fallen on the surgeon's shoulder. Capron was always a handsome, soldierly looking man—some said that he was the most soldierly looking of any of the young officers in the army—and as I saw him then death had given him a great dignity and nobleness. He was only twenty-eight years old, the age when life has just begun, but he rested his head on the surgeon's shoulder like a man who knew he was already through with it and that, though they might peck and mend at the body, he had received his final orders. His breast and shoulders were bare, and as the surgeon cut the tunic from him the sight of his great chest and the skin, as white as a girl's, and the black open wound against it made the yellow stripes and the brass insignia on the tunic, strangely mean and tawdry.

Fifty yards farther on, around a turn in the trail, behind a rock, a boy was lying with a bullet wound between his eyes. His chest was heaving with short, hoarse noises which I guessed were due to some muscular action entirely, and that he was virtually dead. I lifted him and gave him some water, but it would not pass through his fixed teeth. In the pocket of his blouse was a New Testament with the name *Fielder Dawson, Mo.*, scribbled in it in pencil. While I was writing it down for identification, a boy as young as himself came from behind me down the trail.

"It is no use," he said; "the surgeon has seen him; he says he is just the same as dead. He is my bunkie; we only met two weeks ago at San Antonio; but he and me had got to be such good friends—But there's nothing I can do now." He threw himself down on the rock beside his bunkie, who was still breathing with that hoarse inhuman rattle, and I left them, the one who had been spared looking down helplessly with the tears creeping across his cheeks.

The firing was quite close now, and the trail was no longer filled with blanket rolls and haversacks, nor did pitiful, prostrate figures lie in wait behind each rock. I guessed this must mean that I now was well in advance of the farthest point to which Capron's troop had moved, and I was running forward feeling confident that I must be close on our men, when I saw the body of a sergeant blocking the trail and stretched at full length across it. Its position was a hundred yards in advance of that of any of the others—it was apparently the body of the first man killed. After death the bodies of some men seem to shrink almost instantly within themselves; they become limp and shapeless, and their uniforms hang upon them strangely.

But this man, who was a giant in life, remained a giant in death—his very attitude was one of attack; his fists were clinched, his jaw set, and his eyes, which were still human, seemed fixed with resolve. He was dead, but he was not defeated. And so, Hamilton Fish died as he had lived—defiantly, running into the very face of the enemy, standing squarely upright on his legs instead of crouching, as the others called to him to do, until he fell like a column across the trail. "God gives," was the motto on the watch I took from his blouse, and God could not have given him a nobler end; to die, in the fore-front of the first fight of the war, quickly, painlessly, with a bullet through the heart, with his regiment behind him, and facing the enemies of his country.

The line at this time was divided by the trail into two wings. The right wing, composed of K and A Troops, was advancing through the valley, returning the fire from the ridge as it did so, and the left wing, which was much the longer of the two, was swinging around on the enemy's right flank, with its own right resting on the barbed-wire fence. I borrowed a carbine from a wounded man, and joined the remnant of L Troop which was close to the trail.

This troop was then commanded by Second Lieutenant Day, who on account of his conduct that morning and at the battle of San Juan later, when he was shot through the arm, was promoted to be captain of L Troop, or, as it was later officially designated, Capron's troop. He was walking up and down the line as unconcernedly as though we were at target practice, and an Irish sergeant, Byrne, was assisting him by keeping up a continuous flow of comments and criticisms that showed the keenest enjoyment of the situation. Byrne was the only man I noticed who seemed to regard the fight as in any way humorous. For at Guasimas, no one had time to be flippant, or to exhibit any signs of braggadocio. It was for all of them, from the moment it started, through the hot, exhausting hour and a half that it lasted, a most serious proposition.

The conditions were exceptional. The men had made a night march the evening before, had been given but three hours' troubled sleep on the wet sand, and had then been marched in full equipment uphill and under a cruelly hot sun, directly into action. And eighty *per cent.* of them had never before been under fire. Nor had one man in the regiment ever fired a Krag-Jorgensen carbine until he fired it at a Spaniard, for their arms had been issued to them so soon before sailing that they had only drilled with them without using cartridges. To this handicap was also added the nature of the ground and the fact that our men could not see their opponents. Their own men fell or rolled over on every side, shot down by an invisible enemy, with no one upon whom they could retaliate, with no sign that the attack might not go on indefinitely.

Yet they never once took a step backward, but advanced grimly, cleaning a bush or thicket of its occupants before charging it, and securing its cover for themselves, and answering each volley with one that sounded like an echo of the first. The men were panting for

Wounded Rough Riders coming over the hill at Siboney. Head of column of Second Infantry going to support the Rough Riders, June 24th

breath; the sweat ran so readily into their eyes that they could not see the sights of their guns; their limbs unused to such exertion after seven days of cramped idleness on the troop-ship, trembled with weakness and the sun blinded and dazzled them; but time after time they rose and staggered forward through the high grass, or beat their way with their carbines against the tangle of vines and creepers.

A mile and a half of territory was gained foot by foot in this fashion, the three Spanish positions carried in that distance being marked by the thousands of Mauser cartridges that lay shining and glittering in the grass and behind the barricades of bushes. But this distance had not been gained without many losses, for everyone in the regiment was engaged. Even those who, on account of the heat, had dropped out along the trail, as soon as the sound of the fight reached them, came limping to the front—and plunged into the firing-line. It was the only place they could go—there was no other line. With the exception of Church's dressing station and its wounded there were no reserves.

Among the first to be wounded was the correspondent, Edward Marshall, of the New York *Journal*, who was on the firing-line to the left. He was shot through the body near the spine, and when I saw him, he was suffering the most terrible agonies, and passing through a succession of convulsions. He nevertheless, in his brief moments of comparative peace, bore himself with the utmost calm, and was so much a soldier to duty that he continued writing his account of the fight until the fight itself was ended. His courage was the admiration of all the troopers, and he was highly commended by Colonel Wood in the official account of the engagement.

Nothing so well illustrated how desperately each man was needed, and how little was his desire to withdraw, as the fact that the wounded lay where they fell until the hospital stewards found them. Their comrades did not use them as an excuse to go to leave the firing-line. I have watched other fights, where the men engaged were quite willing to unselfishly bear the wounded from the zone of danger.

The fight had now lasted an hour, and the line had reached a more open country, with a slight incline upward toward a wood, on the edge of which was a ruined house. This house was a former distillery for *aguardiente*, and was now occupied in force by the enemy. Lieutenant-Colonel Roosevelt on the far left was moving up his men with the intention of taking this house on the flank; Wood, who was all over the line, had the same objective point in his mind. The troop commanders had a general idea that the distillery was the key to the enemy's position, and were all working in that direction. It was extremely difficult for Wood and Roosevelt to communicate with the captains, and after the first general orders had been given them, they relied upon the latter's intelligence to pull them through. I do not suppose Wood, out of the five hundred engaged, saw more than thirty of his men at any one time.

When he had passed one troop, except for the noise of its volley firing, it was immediately lost to him in the brush, and it was so with the next. Still, so excellent was the intelligence of the officers, and so ready the spirit of the men, that they kept an almost perfect alignment, as was shown when the final order came to charge in the open fields. The advance upon the ruined building was made in stubborn, short rushes, sometimes in silence, and sometimes firing as we ran. The order to fire at will was seldom given, the men waiting patiently for the officers' signal, and then answering in volleys. Some of the men who were twice Day's age begged him to let them take the enemy's impromptu fort on the run, but he answered them tolerantly like spoiled children, and held them down until there was a lull in the enemy's fire, when he would lead them forward, always taking the advance himself.

By the way they made these rushes, it was easy to tell which men were used to hunting big game in the West and which were not. The Eastern men broke at the word, and ran for the cover they were directed to take like men trying to get out of the rain, and fell panting on their faces, while the Western trappers and hunters slipped and wriggled through the grass like Indians; dodging from tree trunk to tree trunk, and from one bush to another. They fell into line at the same time with the others, but while doing so they had not once exposed themselves. Some of the escapes were little short of miraculous. The man on my right, Champneys Marshall, of Washington, had one bullet pass through his sleeve, and another pass through his shirt, where it was pulled close to his spine. The holes where the ball entered and went out again were clearly cut.

Another man's skin was slightly burned by three bullets in three distinct lines, as though it had been touched for an instant by the lighted end of a cigar. Greenway was shot through this shirt across the breast, and Roosevelt was so close to one bullet, when it struck a tree, that it filled his eyes and ears with tiny splinters. Major Brodie and Lieutenant Thomas were both wounded within a few feet of Colonel Wood, and his colour-sergeant, Wright, who followed close at his heels, was clipped three times in the head and neck, and four bullets passed through the folds of the flag he carried. One trooper, Rowland, of Deming, was shot through the lower ribs; he was ordered by Roosevelt to fall back to the dressing station, but there Church told him there was nothing he could do for him then, and directed him to sit down until he could be taken to the hospital at Siboney. Rowland sat still for a short time, and then remarked restlessly, "I don't seem to be doing much good here," and picking up his carbine, returned to the firing-line. There Roosevelt found him.

"I thought I ordered you to the rear," he demanded.

"Yes, sir, you did," Rowland said, "but there didn't seem to be much doing back there."

After the fight he was sent to Siboney with the rest of the wounded, but two days later he appeared in camp. He had marched from Siboney, a distance of six miles, and uphill all the way, carrying his carbine, canteen, and cartridge-belt.

"I thought you were in hospital," Wood said. "I was," Rowland answered sheepishly, "but I didn't seem to be doing any good there."

They gave him up as hopeless, and he continued his duties and went into the fight of the San Juan hills with the hole still through his ribs. Another cowboy named Heffner, when shot through the body, asked to be propped up against a tree with his canteen and cartridge-belt beside him, and the last his troop saw of him he was seated alone grimly firing over their heads in the direction of the enemy.

Early in the fight I came upon Church attending to a young cowboy, who was shot through the chest. The entrance to his wound was so small that Church could not insert enough of the gauze packing to stop the flow of blood

"I'm afraid I'll have to make this hole larger," he said to the boy, "or you'll bleed to death."

"All right," the trooper answered, "I guess you know your business." The boy stretched out on his back and lay perfectly quiet while Church, with a pair of curved scissors, cut away the edges of the wound. His patient neither whimpered nor swore, but stared up at the sun in silence. The bullets were falling on every side, and the operation was a hasty one, but the trooper made no comment until Church said, "We'd better get out of this; can you stand being carried?"

"Do you think you can carry me?" the trooper asked.

"Yes."

"Well," exclaimed the boy admiringly, "you certainly know your business!"

Another of the Rough Riders was brought to the dressing station with a shattered ankle, and Church, after bandaging it, gave him his choice of riding down to Siboney on a mule, or of being carried, a day later, on a litter.

"If you think you can manage to ride the mule with that broken foot," he said, "you can start at once, but if you wait until tomorrow, when I can spare the men, you can be carried all the way."

The cowboy preferred to start at once, so six hospital stewards lifted him and dropped him on the mule, and into a huge Mexican saddle.

He stuck his wounded ankle into one stirrup, and his untouched one into the other, and gathered up the reins.

"Does it pain you? Can you stand it?" Church asked anxiously. The cowboy turned and smiled down upon him with amused disdain.

"Stand *this*?" he cried. "Why, this is just like getting money from home."

Toward the last, the firing from the enemy sounded less near, and the bullets passed much higher. Roosevelt, who had picked up a carbine and was firing to give the direction to the others, determined upon a charge. Wood, at the other end of the line, decided at the same time upon the same manoeuvre. It was called "Wood's bluff" afterward, for he had nothing to back it with; while to the enemy it looked as though his whole force was but the skirmish-line in advance of a regiment. The Spaniards naturally could not believe that this thin line which suddenly broke out of the bushes and from behind trees and came cheering out into the hot sunlight was the entire fighting force against it. They supposed the regiment was coming close on its heels, and as Spanish troops hate being rushed as a cat hates water, they fired a few parting volleys and broke and ran. The cheering had the same invigorating effect on our own side as a cold shower; it was what first told half the men where the other half were, and it made every individual man feel better. As we knew it was only a bluff, the first cheer was wavering, but the sound of our own voices was so comforting that the second cheer was a howl of triumph.

As it was, the Spaniards thought the Rough Riders had already disregarded all the rules of war.

"When we fired a volley," one of the prisoners said later, "instead of falling back they came forward. That is not the way to fight, to come closer at every volley." And so, when instead of retreating on each volley, the Rough Riders rushed at them, cheering and filling the hot air with wild cowboy yells, the dismayed enemy retreated upon Santiago, where he announced he had been attacked by the entire American army.

One of the residents of Santiago asked one of the soldiers if those Americans fought well.

"*Well!*" he replied, "they tried to catch us with their hands!"

I have not attempted to give any account of General Young's fight on our right, which was equally desperate, and, owing to the courage of the coloured troops of the Tenth in storming a ridge, equally worthy of praise. But it has seemed better not to try and tell of anything I did not see, but to limit myself to the work of the Rough Riders, to whom, after all, the victory was due, as it was owing to Colonel Wood's charge, which took the Spaniards in flank, that General Wheeler and General Young were able to advance, their own stubborn attack in front having failed to dislodge the enemy from his rifle-pits.

According to the statement of the enemy, who had every reason not to exaggerate the size of his own force, 4,000 Spaniards were engaged in this action. The Rough Riders numbered 534, and General Young's force numbered 464. The American troops accordingly attacked a force over four times their own number intrenched behind rifle-pits and bushes in a mountain pass. In spite of the smokeless powder used by the Spaniards, which hid their position, the Rough Riders routed them out of it, and drove them back from three different barricades until they made their last stand in the ruined distillery, whence they finally drove them by assault. The eager spirit in which this was accomplished is best described in the Spanish soldier's answer to the inquiring civilian, "They tried to catch us with their hands." The Rough Riders should adopt it as their motto.

The Battle of San Juan Hill

After the Guasimas fight on June 24, the army was advanced along the single trail which leads from Siboney on the coast to Santiago. Two streams of excellent water run parallel with this trail for short distances, and some eight miles from the coast crossed it in two places. Our outposts were stationed at the first of these fords, the Cuban outposts a mile and a half farther on at the ford nearer Santiago, where the stream made a sharp turn at a place called El Poso. Another mile and a half of trail extended from El Poso to the trenches of San Juan. The reader should remember El Poso, as it marked an important starting-point against San Juan on the eventful first of July.

For six days the army was encamped on either side of the trail for three miles back from the outposts. The regimental camps touched each other, and all day long the pack-trains carrying the day's rations passed up and down between them. The trail was a sunken wagon road, where it was possible, in a few places, for two wagons to pass at one time, but the greater distances were so narrow that there was but just room for a wagon, or a loaded mule-train, to make its way. The banks of the trail were three or four feet high, and when it rained it was converted into a huge gutter, with sides of mud, and with a liquid mud a foot deep between them.

The camps were pitched along the trail as near the parallel stream as possible, and in the occasional places where there was rich, high grass. At night the men slept in dog tents, open at the front and back, and during the day spent their time under the shade of trees along the trail, or on the banks of the stream. Sentries were placed at every few feet along these streams to guard them from any possible pollution. For six days the army rested in this way, for as an army moves and acts only on its belly, and as the belly of this army was three miles long, it could advance but slowly.

This week of rest, after the cramped life of the troop-ship, was not ungrateful, although the rations were scarce and there was no tobacco, which was as necessary to the health of the men as their food.

During this week of waiting, the chief excitement was to walk out a mile and a half beyond the outposts to the hill of El Poso, and look across the basin that lay in the great valley which leads to Santiago. The left of the valley was the hills which hide the sea. The right of the valley was the hills in which nestle the village of El Caney. Below El Poso, in the basin, the dense green forest stretched a mile and a half to the hills of San Juan. These hills looked so quiet and sunny and well-kept that they reminded one of a New England orchard. There was a blue bungalow on a hill to the right, a red bungalow higher up on the right, and in the centre the blockhouse of San Juan, which looked like a Chinese *pagoda*. Three-quarters of a mile behind them, with a dip between, were the long white walls of the hospital and barracks of Santiago, wearing thirteen Red Cross flags, and, as was pointed out to the foreign *attachés* later, two six-inch guns a hundred yards in advance of the Red Cross flags.

It was so quiet, so fair, and so prosperous looking that it breathed of peace. It seemed as though one might, without accident, walk in and take dinner at the Venus Restaurant, or loll on the benches in the *Plaza*, or rock in one of the great bent-wood chairs around the patio of the Don Carlos Club.

But, on the 27th of June, a long, yellow pit opened in the hill-side of San Juan, and in it we could see straw *sombreros* rising and bobbing up and down, and under the shade of the blockhouse, blue-coated Spaniards strolling leisurely about or riding forth on little white ponies to scamper over the hills. Officers of every regiment, *attachés* of foreign countries, correspondents, and staff officers daily reported the fact that the rifle-pits were growing in length and in number, and that in plain sight from the hill of El Poso the enemy was intrenching himself at San Juan, and at the little village of El Caney to the right, where he was marching through the streets. But no artillery was sent to El Poso hill to drop a shell among the busy men at work among the trenches, or to interrupt the street parades in El Caney. For four days before the American soldiers captured the same rifle-pits at El Caney and San Juan, with a loss of two thousand men, they watched these men diligently preparing for their coming, and wondered why there was no order to embarrass or to end these preparations.

On the afternoon of June 30, Captain Mills rode up to the tent of Colonel Wood, and told him that on account of illness, General Wheeler and General Young had relinquished their commands, and that General Sumner would take charge of the cavalry division; that he, Colonel Wood, would take command of General Young's brigade, and Colonel Carroll, of General Sumner's brigade.

"You will break camp and move forward at four o'clock," he said. It was then three o'clock, and apparently the order to move forward at four had been given to each regiment at nearly the same time, for they all struck their tents and stepped down into the trail together. It was as though fifteen regiments were encamped along the sidewalks of Fifth Avenue and were all ordered at the same moment to move into it and march downtown. If Fifth Avenue were ten feet wide, one can imagine the confusion.

General Chaffee was at General Lawton's headquarters, and they stood apart whispering together about the march they were to take to El Caney. Just over their heads the balloon was ascending for the first time and its great glistening bulk hung just above the tree tops, and the men in different regiments, picking their way along the trail, gazed up at it open-mouthed. The headquarters camp was crowded. After a week of inaction, the army, at a moment's notice, was moving forward, and every one had ridden in haste to learn why.

There were *attachés*, in strange uniforms, self-important Cuban generals, officers from the flagship *New York*, and an army of photographers. At the side of the camp, double lines of soldiers passed slowly along the two paths of the muddy road, while, between them, *aides* dashed up and down, splashing them with dirty water, and shouting, "You will come up at once, sir." "You will not attempt to enter the trail yet, sir." "General Sumner's compliments, and why are you not in your place?"

Twelve thousand men, with their eyes fixed on a balloon, and treading on each other's heels in three inches of mud, move slowly, and after three hours, it seemed as though every man in the United States was under arms and stumbling and slipping down that trail. The lines passed until the moon rose. They seemed endless, interminable; there were cavalry mounted and dismounted, artillery with cracking whips and cursing drivers, Rough Riders in brown, and regulars, both black and white, in blue. Midnight came, and they were still stumbling and slipping forward.

General Sumner's headquarters tent was pitched to the right of El Poso hill. Below us lay the basin a mile and a half in length, and a mile and a half wide, from which a white mist was rising. Near us, drowned under the mist, seven thousand men were sleeping, and, farther to the right, General Chaffee's five thousand were lying under the bushes along the trails to El Caney, waiting to march on it and eat it up before breakfast.

The place hardly needs a map to explain it. The trails were like a pitchfork, with its prongs touching the hills of San Juan. The long handle of the pitchfork was the trail over which we had just come, the joining of the handle and the prongs were El Poso. El Caney lay half-way along the right prong the left one was the trail down which, in the morning, the troops were to be hurled upon San Juan. It was as yet an utterly undiscovered country. Three miles away, across the basin of mist, we could see the street lamps of Santiago shining over the San Juan hills. Above us, the tropical moon hung white and clear in the dark purple sky, pierced with millions of white stars.

As we turned in, there was just a little something in the air which made saying "goodnight" a gentle farce, for no one went to sleep immediately, but lay looking up at the stars, and after a long silence, and much restless turning on the blanket which we shared together, the second lieutenant said: "So, if anything happens to me, tomorrow, you'll see she gets them, won't you?" Before the moon rose again, every sixth man who had slept in the mist that night was either killed or wounded; but the second lieutenant was sitting on the edge of a Spanish rifle-pit, dirty, sweaty, and weak for food, but victorious, and the unknown she did not get them.

El Caney had not yet thrown off her blanket of mist before Capron's battery opened on it from a ridge two miles in the rear. The plan for the day was that El Caney should fall in an hour. The plan for the day is interesting chiefly because it is so different from what happened. According to the plan the army was to advance in two divisions along the two trails. Incidentally, General Lawton's division was to pick up El Caney, and when El Caney was eliminated, his division was to continue forward and join hands on the right with the divisions of General Sumner and General Kent. The army was then to rest for that night in the woods, half a mile from San Juan.

On the following morning it was to attack San Juan on the two flanks, under cover of artillery. The objection to this plan, which did not apparently suggest itself to General Shafter, was that an army of twelve thousand men, sleeping within five hundred yards of the enemy's rifle-pits, might not unreasonably be expected to pass a bad night. As we discovered the next day, not only the five hundred yards, but the whole basin was covered by the fire from the rifle-pits. Even by daylight, when it was possible to seek some slight shelter, the army could not remain in the woods, but according to the plan it was expected to bivouac for the night in those woods, and in the morning to manoeuvre and deploy and march through them to the two flanks of San Juan. How the enemy was to be hypnotised while this was going forward it is difficult to understand.

According to this programme, Capron's battery opened on El Caney and Grimes's battery opened on the *pagoda*-like blockhouse of San Juan. The range from El Poso was exactly 2,400 yards, and the firing, as was discovered later, was not very effective. The battery used black powder, and, as a result, after each explosion the curtain of smoke hung over the gun for fully a minute before the gunners could see the San Juan trenches, which was chiefly important because for a full minute it gave a mark to the enemy. The hill on which the battery stood was like a sugar-loaf. Behind it was the farmhouse of El Poso, the only building in sight within a radius of a mile, and in it were Cuban soldiers and other non-combatants. The Rough Riders had been ordered to halt in the yard of the farmhouse and the artillery horses were drawn up in it, under the lee of the hill.

The First and Tenth dismounted cavalry were encamped a hundred yards from the battery along the ridge. They might as sensibly have been ordered to paint the rings in a target while a company was firing at the bull's-eye. To our first twenty shots the enemy made no reply; when they did it was impossible, owing to their using smokeless powder, to locate their guns. Their third shell fell in among the Cubans in the blockhouse and among the Rough Riders and the men of the First and Tenth Cavalry, killing some and wounding many. These casualties were utterly unnecessary and were due to the stupidity of whoever placed the men within fifty yards of guns in action.

A quarter of an hour after the firing began from El Poso one of General Shafter's *aides* directed General Sumner to advance with his division down the Santiago trail, and to halt at the edge of the woods.

"What am I to do then?" asked General Sumner.

"You are to await further orders," the *aide* answered.

As a matter of fact and history this was probably the last order General Sumner received from General Shafter, until the troops of his division had taken the San Juan hills, as it became impossible to get word to General Shafter, the trail leading to his headquarters tent,

Grimes's battery at El Poso

The third Spanish shell fell in among the Cubans in the block-house and among the Rough Riders three miles in the rear, being blocked by the soldiers of the First and Tenth dismounted cavalry, and later, by Lawton's division. General Sumner led the Sixth, Third, and Ninth Cavalry and the Rough Riders down the trail, with instructions for the First and Tenth to follow. The trail, virgin as yet from the foot of an American soldier, was as wide as its narrowest part, which was some ten feet across. At places it was as wide as Broadway, but only for such short distances that it was necessary for the men to advance in column, in double file.

A maze of underbrush and trees on either side was all but impenetrable, and when the officers and men had once assembled into the basin, they could only guess as to what lay before them, or on either flank. At the end of a mile the country became more open, and General Sumner saw the Spaniards intrenched a half-mile away on the sloping hills. A stream, called the San Juan River, ran across the trail at this point, and another stream crossed it again two hundred yards farther on. The troops were halted at this first stream, some crossing it, and others deploying in single file to the right. Some were on the banks of the stream, others at the edge of the woods in the bushes. Others lay in the high grass which was so high that it stopped the wind, and so hot that it almost choked and suffocated those who lay in it.

The enemy saw the advance and began firing with pitiless accuracy into the jammed and crowded trail and along the whole border of the woods. There was not a single yard of ground for a mile to the rear which was not inside the zone of fire. Our men were ordered not to return the fire but to lie still and wait for further orders. Some of them could see the rifle-pits of the enemy quite clearly and the men in them, but many saw nothing but the bushes under which they lay, and the high grass which seemed to burn when they pressed against it. It was during this period of waiting that the greater number of our men were killed. For one hour they lay on their rifles staring at the waving green stuff around them, while the bullets drove past incessantly, with savage insistence, cutting the grass again and again in hundreds of fresh places.

Men in line sprang from the ground and sank back again with a groan, or rolled to one side clinging silently to an arm or shoulder. Behind the line's hospital stewards passed continually, drawing the wounded back to the streams, where they laid them in long rows, their feet touching the water's edge and their bodies supported by the muddy bank. Up and down the lines, and through the fords of the streams, mounted *aides* drove their horses at a gallop, as conspicuous a target as the steeple on a church, and one after another paid the price of his position and fell from his horse wounded or dead. Captain Mills fell as he was giving an order, shot through the forehead behind both eyes; Captain O'Neill, of the Rough Riders, as he said, "There is no Spanish bullet made that can kill me." Steel, Swift, Henry, each of them was shot out of his saddle.

Hidden in the trees above the streams, and above the trail, sharp-shooters and guerillas added a fresh terror to the wounded. There was no hiding from them. Their bullets came from every side. Their invisible smoke helped to keep their hiding-places secret, and in the incessant shriek of shrapnel and the spit of the Mausers, it was difficult to locate the reports of their rifles. They spared neither the wounded nor recognised the Red Cross; they killed the surgeons and the stewards carrying the litters, and killed the wounded men on the litters. A guerilla in a tree above us shot one of the Rough Riders in the breast while I was helping him carry Captain Morton Henry to the dressing-station, the ball passing down through him, and a second shot, from the same tree, barely missed Henry as he lay on the ground where we had dropped him. He was already twice wounded and so covered with blood that no one could have mistaken his condition.

The surgeons at work along the stream dressed the wounds with one eye cast aloft at the trees. It was not the Mauser bullets they feared, though they passed continuously, but too high to do their patients further harm, but the bullets of the sharpshooters which struck fairly in among them, splashing in the water and scattering the pebbles. The sounds of the two bullets were as different as is the sharp pop of a soda-water bottle from the buzzing of an angry wasp.

For a time it seemed as though every second man was either killed or wounded; one came upon them lying behind the bush, under which they had crawled with some strange idea that it would protect them, or crouched under the bank of the stream, or lying on their stomachs and lapping up the water with the eagerness of thirsty dogs. As to their suffering, the wounded were magnificently silent, they neither complained nor groaned nor cursed.

"I've got a punctured tyre," was their grim answer to inquiries. White men and coloured men, veterans and recruits and volunteers, each lay waiting for the battle to begin or to end so that he might be carried away to safety, for the wounded were in as great danger after they were hit as though they were in the firing line, but none questioned nor complained.

I came across Lieutenant Roberts, of the Tenth Cavalry, lying under the roots of a tree beside the stream with three of his coloured troopers stretched around him. He was shot through the intestines, and each of the three men with him was shot in the arm or leg. They had been overlooked or forgotten, and we stumbled upon them only by the accident of losing our way. They had no knowledge as to how the battle was going or where their comrades were or where the enemy was. At any moment, for all they knew, the Spaniards might break through the bushes about them.

It was a most lonely picture, the young lieutenant, half naked, and wet with his own blood, sitting upright beside the empty stream, and his three followers crouching at his feet like three faithful watchdogs, each wearing his red badge of courage, with his black skin tanned to a haggard grey, and with his eyes fixed patiently on the white lips of his officer. When the white soldiers with me offered to carry him back to the dressing-station, the negroes resented it stiffly. "If the lieutenant had been able to move, we would have carried him away long ago," said the sergeant, quite overlooking the fact that his arm was shattered.

"Oh, don't bother the surgeons about me," Roberts added, cheerfully. "They must be very busy. I can wait."

As yet, with all these killed and wounded, we had accomplished nothing—except to obey orders—which was to await further orders. The observation balloon hastened the end. It came blundering down the trail, and stopped the advance of the First and Tenth Cavalry, and was sent up directly over the heads of our men to observe what should have been observed a week before by scouts and reconnoitring parties. A balloon, two miles to the rear, and high enough in the air to be out of range of the enemy's fire may someday prove itself to be of use and value. But a balloon on the advance line, and only fifty feet above the tops of the trees, was merely an invitation to the enemy to kill everything beneath it. And the enemy responded to the invitation. A Spaniard might question if he could hit a man, or a number of men, hidden in the bushes, but had no doubt at all as to his ability to hit a mammoth glistening ball only six hundred yards distant, and so all the trenches fired at it at once, and the men of the First and Tenth, packed together directly behind it, received the full force of the bullets.

The men lying directly below it received the shrapnel which was timed to hit it, and which at last, fortunately, did hit it. This was endured for an hour, an hour of such hell of fire and heat, that the heat in itself, had there been no bullets, would have been remembered for its cruelty. Men gasped on their backs, like fishes in the bottom of a boat, their heads burning inside and out, their limbs too heavy to move. They had been rushed here and rushed there wet with sweat and wet with fording the streams, under a sun that would have made moving a fan an effort, and they lay prostrate, gasping at the hot air, with faces aflame, and their tongues sticking out, and their eyes rolling. All through this the volleys from the rifle-pits sputtered and rattled, and the bullets sang continuously like the wind through the rigging in a gale, shrapnel whined and broke, and still no order came from General Shafter.

Captain Howse, of General Sumner's staff, rode down the trail to learn what had delayed the First and Tenth, and was hailed by Colonel Derby, who was just descending from the shattered balloon.

"I saw men up there on those hills," Colonel Derby shouted; "they are firing at our troops." That was part of the information contributed by the balloon. Captain Howse's reply is lost to history.

General Kent's division, which, according to the plan, was to have been held in reserve, had been rushed up in the rear of the First and Tenth, and the Tenth had deployed in skirmish order to the right. The trail was now completely blocked by Kent's division. Lawton's division, which was to have re-enforced on the right, had not appeared, but incessant firing from the direction of El Caney showed that he and Chaffee were fighting mightily. The situation was desperate. Our troops could not retreat, as the trail for two miles behind them was wedged with men. They could not remain where they were, for they were being shot to pieces. There was only one thing they could do— go forward and take the San Juan hills by assault. It was as desperate as the situation itself.

To charge earthworks held by men with modern rifles, and using modern artillery, until after the earthworks have been shaken by artillery, and to attack them in advance and not in the flanks, are both impossible military propositions. But this campaign had not been conducted according to military rules, and a series of military blunders had brought seven thousand American soldiers into a chute of death from which there was no escape except by taking the enemy who held it by the throat and driving him out and beating him down. So the generals of divisions and brigades stepped back and relinquished their command to the regimental officers and the enlisted men.

"We can do nothing more," they virtually said. "There is the enemy."

Colonel Roosevelt, on horseback, broke from the woods behind the line of the Ninth, and finding its men lying in his way, shouted: "If you don't wish to go forward, let my men pass." The junior officers of the Ninth, with their negroes, instantly sprang into line with the Rough Riders, and charged at the blue blockhouse on the right.

I speak of Roosevelt first because, with General Hawkins, who led Kent's division, notably the Sixth and Sixteenth Regulars, he was, without doubt, the most conspicuous figure in the charge. General Hawkins, with hair as white as snow, and yet far in advance of men thirty years his junior, was so noble a sight that you felt inclined to pray for his safety; on the other hand, Roosevelt, mounted high on horseback, and charging the rifle-pits at a gallop and quite alone, made you feel that you would like to cheer. He wore on his *sombrero* a blue polka-dot handkerchief, à la Havelock, which, as he advanced, floated out straight behind his head, like a guidon.

Afterward, the men of his regiment who followed this flag, adopted a polka-dot handkerchief as the badge of the Rough Riders. These two officers were notably conspicuous in the charge, but no one can claim that any two men, or any one man, was more brave or more daring, or showed greater courage in that slow, stubborn advance, than did any of the others. Someone asked one of the officers if he had any difficulty in making his men follow him.

"No," he answered, "I had some difficulty in keeping up with them."

As one of the brigade generals said: "San Juan was won by the regimental officers and men. We had as little to do as the referee at a prize-fight who calls 'time.' We called 'time' and they did the fighting."

I have seen many illustrations and pictures of this charge on the San Juan hills, but none of them seem to show it just as I remember it. In the picture-papers the men are running uphill swiftly and gallantly, in regular formation, rank after rank, with flags flying, their eyes aflame, and their hair streaming, their bayonets fixed, in long, brilliant lines, an invincible, overpowering weight of numbers. Instead of which I think the thing which impressed one the most, when our men started from cover, was that they were so few. It seemed as if someone had made an awful and terrible mistake. One's instinct was to call to them to come back. You felt that someone had blundered and that these few men were blindly following out some madman's mad order. It was not heroic then, it seemed merely absurdly pathetic. The pity of it, the folly of such a sacrifice was what held you.

They had no glittering bayonets, they were not massed in regular array. There were a few men in advance, bunched together, and creeping up a steep, sunny hill, the tops of which roared and flashed with flame. The men held their guns pressed across their chests and stepped heavily as they climbed. Behind these first few, spreading out like a fan, were single lines of men, slipping and scrambling in the smooth grass, moving forward with difficulty, as though they were wading waist high through water, moving slowly, carefully, with strenuous effort. It was much more wonderful than any swinging charge could have been. They walked to greet death at every step, many of them, as they advanced, sinking suddenly or pitching forward and disappearing in the high grass, but the others waded on, stubbornly, forming a thin blue line that kept creeping higher and higher up the hill.

It was as inevitable as the rising tide. It was a miracle of self-sacrifice, a triumph of bull-dog courage, which one watched breathless with wonder. The fire of the Spanish riflemen, who still stuck bravely to their posts, doubled and trebled in fierceness, the crests of the hills crackled and burst in amazed roars, and rippled with waves of tiny flame. But the blue line crept steadily up and on, and then, near the top, the broken fragments gathered together with a sudden burst of speed, the Spaniards appeared for a moment outlined against the sky and poised for instant flight, fired a last volley, and fled before the swift-moving wave that leaped and sprang after them.

The men of the Ninth and the Rough Riders rushed to the blockhouse together, the men of the Sixth, of the Third, of the Tenth Cavalry, of the Sixth and Sixteenth Infantry, fell on their faces along the crest of the hills beyond, and opened upon the vanishing enemy. They drove the yellow silk flags of the cavalry and the flag of their country into the soft earth of the trenches, and then sank down and looked back at the road they had climbed and swung their hats in the air. And from far overhead, from these few figures perched on the Spanish rifle-pits, with their flags planted among the empty cartridges of the enemy, and overlooking the walls of Santiago, came, faintly, the sound of a tired, broken cheer.

The Taking of Coamo

This is the inside story of the surrender, during the Spanish War, of the town of Coamo. It is written by the man to whom the town surrendered. Immediately after the surrender this same man became Military Governor of Coamo. He held office for fully twenty minutes.

Before beginning this story, the reader must forget all he may happen to know of this particular triumph of the Porto Rican Expedition. He must forget that the taking of Coamo has always been credited to Major-General James H. Wilson, who on that occasion commanded Captain Anderson's Battery, the Sixteenth Pennsylvania, Troop C of Brooklyn, and under General Ernst, the Second and Third Wisconsin Volunteers. He must forget that in the records of the War Department all the praise, and it is of the highest, for this victory is bestowed upon General Wilson and his four thousand soldiers.

Even the writer of this, when he cabled an account of the event to his paper, gave, with everyone else, the entire credit to General Wilson. And ever since his conscience has upbraided him. His only claim for tolerance as a war correspondent has been that he always has stuck to the facts, and now he feels that in the sacred cause of history his friendship and admiration for General Wilson, that veteran of the Civil, Philippine, and Chinese Wars, must no longer stand in the way of his duty as an accurate reporter. He no longer can tell a lie. He must at last own up that he himself captured Coamo.

On the morning of the 9th of August, 1898, the Sixteenth Pennsylvania Volunteers arrived on the outskirts of that town. In order to get there, they had spent the night in crawling over mountain trails and scrambling through streams and ravines. It was General Wilson's plan that by this flanking night march the Sixteenth Pennsylvania would reach the road leading from Coamo to San Juan in time to cut off the retreat of the Spanish garrison, when General Wilson, with the main body, attacked it from the opposite side.

At seven o'clock in the morning General Wilson began the frontal attack by turning loose the artillery on a blockhouse, which threatened his approach, and by advancing the Wisconsin Volunteers. The cavalry he sent to the right to capture Los Baños. At eight o'clock, from where the main body rested, two miles from Coamo, we could hear the Sixteenth Pennsylvania open its attack and instantly become hotly engaged. The enemy returned the fire fiercely, and the firing from both sides at once became so severe that it was evident the Pennsylvania Volunteers either would take the town without the main body, or that they would greatly need its assistance.

The artillery was accordingly advanced one thousand yards and the infantry was hurried forward. The Second Wisconsin approached Coamo along the main road from Ponce, the Third Wisconsin through fields of grass to the right of the road, until the two regiments met at the ford by which the Baños road crosses the Coamo River. But before they met, from a position near the artillery, I had watched through my glasses the Second Wisconsin with General Ernst at its head advancing along the main road, and as, when I saw them, they were near the river, I guessed they would continue across the bridge and that they soon would be in the town.

As the firing from the Sixteenth still continued, it seemed obvious that General Ernst would be the first general officer to enter Coamo, and to receive its surrender. I had never seen five thousand people surrender to one man, and it seemed that, if I were to witness that ceremony, my best plan was to abandon the artillery and, as quickly as possible, pursue the Second Wisconsin. I did not want to share the spectacle of the surrender with my brother correspondents, so I tried to steal away from the three who were present. They were Thomas F. Millard, Walstein Root of the *Sun*, and Horace Thompson. By dodging through a coffee *central* came out a half mile from them and in advance of the Third Wisconsin. There I encountered two "boy officers," Captain John C. Breckenridge and Lieutenant Fred. S. Titus, who had temporarily abandoned their thankless duties in the Commissariat Department in order to seek death or glory in the skirmish-line. They wanted to know where I was going, and when I explained, they declared that when Coamo surrendered they also were going to be among those present.

So, we slipped away from the main body and rode off as an independent organisation. But from the bald ridge, where the artillery

113

Officers watching the artillery play on Coamo

Drawn by F. C. Yohn from a photograph by the Author

was still hammering the town, the three correspondents and Captain Alfred Paget, Her Majesty's Naval *attaché*, observed our attempt to steal a march on General Wilson's forces, and pursued us and soon overtook us.

We now were seven, or to be exact, eight, for with Mr. Millard was "Jimmy," who in times of peace sells papers in Herald Square, and in times of war carries Mr. Millard's copy to the press post. We were much nearer the ford than the bridge, so we waded the "drift" and started on a gallop along the mile of military road that lay between us and Coamo. The firing from the Sixteenth Pennsylvania had slackened, but as we advanced it became sharper, more insistent, and seemed to urge us to greater speed.

Across the road were dug rough rifle-pits which had the look of having been but that moment abandoned. What had been intended for the breakfast of the enemy was burning in pots over tiny fires, little heaps of cartridges lay in readiness upon the edges of each pit, and an armchair, in which a sentry had kept a comfortable lookout, lay sprawling in the middle of the road. The huts that faced it were empty. The only living things we saw were the chickens and pigs in the kitchen-gardens. On either hand was every evidence of hasty and panic-stricken flight. We rejoiced at these evidences of the fact that the Wisconsin Volunteers had swept all before them.

Our rejoicings were not entirely unselfish. It was so quiet ahead that someone suggested the town had already surrendered. But that would have been too bitter a disappointment, and as the firing from the further side of Coamo still continued, we refused to believe it, and whipped the ponies into greater haste. We were now only a quarter of a mile distant from the built-up portion of Coamo, where the road turned sharply into the main street of the town.

Captain Paget, who in the absence of the British Military *attaché* on account of sickness, accompanied the army as a guest of General Wilson, gave way to thoughts of etiquette.

"Will General Wilson think I should have waited for him?" he shouted. The words were jolted out of him as he rose in the saddle. The noise of the ponies' hoofs made conversation difficult. I shouted back that the presence of General Ernst in the town made it quite proper for a foreign *attaché* to enter it.

"It must have surrendered by now," I shouted. "It's been half an hour since Ernst crossed the bridge."

At these innocent words, all my companions tugged violently at their bridles and shouted "Whoa!"

"Crossed the bridge?" they yelled. "There is no bridge! The bridge is blown up! If he hasn't crossed by the ford, he isn't in the town!"

Then, in my turn, I shouted "Whoa!"

But by now the Porto Rican ponies had decided that this was the race of their lives, and each had made up his mind that, Mexican bit or no Mexican bit, until he had carried his rider first into the town of Coamo, he would not be halted. As I tugged helplessly at my Mexican bit, I saw how I had made my mistake. The volunteers, on finding the bridge destroyed, instead of marching upon Coamo had turned to the ford, the same ford which we had crossed half an hour before they reached it. They now were behind us. Instead of a town which had surrendered to a thousand American soldiers, we, seven unarmed men and Jimmy, were being swept into a hostile city as fast as the enemy's ponies could take us there.

Breckenridge and Titus hastily put the blame upon me.

"If we get into trouble with the general for this," they shouted, "it will be your fault. You told us Ernst was in the town with a thousand men."

I shouted back that no one regretted the fact that he was not more keenly than I did myself.

Titus and Breckenridge each glanced at a new, full-dress sword.

"We might as well go in," they shouted, "and take it anyway!" I decided that Titus and Breckenridge were wasted in the Commissariat Department.

The three correspondents looked more comfortable.

"If you officers go in," they cried, "the general can't blame us," and they dug their spurs into the ponies.

"Wait!" shouted Her Majesty's representative. "That's all very well for you chaps, but what protects me if the Admiralty finds out I have led a charge on a Spanish garrison?"

But Paget's pony refused to consider the feelings of the Lords of the Admiralty. As successfully Paget might have tried to pull back a row-boat from the edge of Niagara. And, moreover, Millard, in order that Jimmy might be the first to reach Ponce with despatches, had mounted him on the fastest pony in the bunch, and he already was far in the lead. His sporting instincts, nursed in the pool rooms of the Tenderloin and at Guttenburg, had sent him three lengths to the good. It never would do to have a newsboy tell in New York that he had beaten the correspondents of the papers he sold in the streets; nor to permit commissioned officers to take the dust of one who never before had ridden on anything but a cable car.

So, we all raced forward and, bunched together, swept into the main street of Coamo. It was gratefully empty. There were no American soldiers, but, then, neither were there any Spanish soldiers. Across the street stretched more rifle-pits and barricades of iron pipes, but in sight there was neither friend nor foe. On the stones of the deserted street the galloping hoofs sounded like the advance of a whole regiment of cavalry. Their clatter gave us a most comfortable feeling. We almost could imagine the townspeople believing us to be the Rough Riders themselves and fleeing before us.

And then, the empty street seemed to threaten an ambush. We thought hastily of sunken mines, of soldiers crouching behind the barriers, behind the houses at the next corner, of Mausers covering us from the latticed balconies overhead. Until at last, when the silence had become alert and menacing, a lonely man dashed into the middle of the street, hurled a white flag in front of us, and then dived headlong under the porch of a house. The next instant, as though at a signal, a hundred citizens, each with a white flag in both hands, ran from cover, waving their banners, and gasping in weak and terror-shaken tones, "*Vivan los Americanos.*"

We tried to pull up, but the ponies had not yet settled among themselves which of us had won, and carried us to the extreme edge of the town, where a precipice seemed to invite them to stop, and we fell off into the arms of the Porto Ricans. They brought us wine in tin cans, cigars, borne in the aprons and *mantillas* of their womenfolk, and demijohns of native rum. They were abject, trembling, tearful. They made one instantly forget that the moment before he had been extremely frightened.

One of them spoke to me the few words of Spanish with which I had an acquaintance. He told me he was the *alcalde*, and that he begged to surrender into my hands the town of Coamo. I led him instantly to one side. I was afraid that if I did not take him up, he would surrender to Paget or to Jimmy. I bade him conduct me to his official residence. He did so, and gave me the key to the *cartel*, a staff of office of gold and ebony, and the flag of the town, which he had hidden behind his writing-desk. It was a fine Spanish flag with the coat of arms embroidered in gold. I decided that, with whatever else I might part, that flag would always be mine, that the chance of my again receiving the surrender of a town of five thousand people was slender, and that this token would be wrapped around me in my coffin. I accordingly hid it in my *poncho* and strapped it to my saddle.

Then I appointed a hotel-keeper, who spoke a little English, as my official interpreter, and told the *alcalde* that I was now Military Governor, Mayor, and Chief of Police, and that I wanted the seals of the town. He gave me a rubber stamp with a coat of arms cut in it, and I wrote myself three letters, which, to ensure their safe arrival, I addressed to three different places, and stamped them with the rubber seals. In time all three reached me, and I now have them as documentary proof of the fact that for twenty minutes I was Military Governor and Mayor of Coamo.

During that brief administration I detailed Titus and Breckenridge to wigwag the Sixteenth Pennsylvania that we had taken the town, and that it was now safe for them to enter. In order to compromise Paget, they used his red silk handkerchief. Root I detailed to conciliate the inhabitants by drinking with every one of them. He tells me he carried out my instructions to the letter. I also settled one assault and battery case, and put the chief offender under arrest. At least, I told the official interpreter to inform him that he was under arrest, but as I had no one to guard him he grew tired of being under arrest and went off to celebrate his emancipation from the rule of Spain.

My administration came to an end in twenty minutes, when General Wilson rode into Coamo at the head of his staff and three thousand men. He wore a white helmet, and he looked the part of the conquering hero so satisfactorily that I forgot I was mayor and ran out into the street to snap a picture of him. He looked greatly surprised and asked me what I was doing in his town. The tone in which he spoke caused me to decide that, after all, I would not keep the flag of Coamo. I pulled it off my saddle and said: "General, it's too long a story to tell you now, but here is the flag of the town. It's the first Spanish flag"—and it was—"that has been captured in Porto Rico."

General Wilson smiled again and accepted the flag. He and about four thousand other soldiers think it belongs to them. But the truth will out. Someday the bestowal on the proper persons of a vote of thanks from Congress, a pension, or any other trifle, like prize-money, will show the American people to whom that flag really belongs.

I know that in time the glorious deed of the seven heroes of Coamo, or eight, if you include "Jimmy," will be told in song and story. Someone else will write the song. This is the story.

The Passing of San Juan Hill

When I was a boy, I thought battles were fought in waste places selected for the purpose. I argued from the fact that when our school nine wished to play ball it was forced into the suburbs to search for a vacant lot. I thought opposing armies also marched out of town until they reached some desolate spot where there were no window panes, and where their cannon-balls would hurt no one but themselves. Even later, when I saw battles fought among villages, artillery galloping through a cornfield, garden walls breached for rifle fire, and farmhouses in flames, it always seemed as though the generals had elected to fight in such surroundings through an inexcusable striving after theatrical effect—as though they wished to furnish the war correspondents with a chance for descriptive writing. With the horrors of war as horrible as they are without any aid from these contrasts, their presence always seemed not only sinful but bad art; as unnecessary as turning a red light on the dying gladiator.

There are so many places which are scenes set apart for battles—places that look as though Nature had condemned them for just such sacrifices. Colenso, with its bare *kopjes* and great stretch of *veldt*, is one of these, and so, also, is Spion Kop, and, in Manchuria, Nan Shan Hill. The photographs have made all of us familiar with the vast, desolate approaches to Port Arthur. These are among the waste places of the earth—barren, deserted, fit meeting grounds only for men whose object in life for the moment is to kill men. Were you shown over one of these places, and told, "A battle was fought here," you would answer, "Why, of course!"

But down in Cuba, outside of Santiago, where the United States Army fought its solitary and modest battle with Spain, you might many times pass by San Juan Hill and think of it, if you thought of it at all, as only a pretty site for a bungalow, as a place obviously intended for orchards and gardens.

On July 1st, twelve years ago, when the American Army came upon it out of the jungle the place wore a partial disguise. It still was an irregular ridge of smiling, sunny hills with fat, comfortable curves, and in some places a steep, straight front. But above the steepest, highest front frowned an aggressive blockhouse, and on all the slopes and along the sky-line were rows of yellow trenches, and at the base a cruel cat's cradle of barbed wire. It was like the face of a pretty woman behind the bars of a visor. I find that on the day of the fight twelve years ago I cabled my paper that San Juan Hill reminded the Americans of "a sunny orchard in New England." That was how it may have looked when the regulars were climbing up the steep front to capture the blockhouse, and when the cavalry and Rough Riders, having taken Kettle Hill, were running down its opposite slope, past the lake, to take that crest of San Juan Hill which lies to the right of the blockhouse.

It may then have looked like a sunny New England orchard, but before night fell the intrenching tools had lent those sunny slopes "a fierce and terrible aspect." And after that, hour after hour, and day after day, we saw the hill eaten up by our trenches, hidden by a vast laundry of shelter tents, and torn apart by bomb-proofs, their jutting roofs of logs and broken branches weighed down by earth and stones and looking like the pit mouths to many mines. That probably is how most of the American Army last saw San Juan Hill, and that probably is how it best remembers it—as a fortified camp. That was twelve years ago. When I revisited it, San Juan Hill was again a sunny, smiling farmland, the trenches planted with vegetables, the roofs of the bomb-proofs fallen in and buried beneath creeping vines, and the barbed-wire entanglements holding in check only the browsing cattle.

San Juan Hill is not a solitary hill, but the most prominent of a ridge of hills, with Kettle Hill a quarter of a mile away on the edge of the jungle and separated from the ridge by a tiny lake. In the local nomenclature Kettle Hill, which is the name given to it by the Rough Riders, has always been known as San Juan Hill, with an added name to distinguish it from the other San Juan Hill of greater renown.

The days we spent on those hills were so rich in incident and interest and were filled with moments of such excitement, of such pride in one's fellow-countrymen, of pity for the hurt and dying, of laughter and good-fellowship, that one supposed he might return after even twenty years and recognise every detail of the ground. But a shorter time has made startling and confusing changes. Now a visitor will find that not until after several different visits, and by walking and riding foot by foot over the hills, can he make them fall into line as he thinks he once knew them. Immediately around San Juan Hill itself there has been some attempt made to preserve the ground as a public park. A barbed-wire fence, with a gateway, encircles the blockhouse, which has been converted into a home for the caretaker of the park, and then, skirting the road to Santiago to include the tree under which the surrender was arranged, stretches to the left of the blockhouse to protect a monument.

This monument was erected by Americans to commemorate the battle. It is now rapidly falling to pieces, but there still is enough of it intact to show the pencilled scribblings and autographs of tourists who did not take part in the battle, but who in this public manner show that they approve of its results. The public park is less than a quarter of a mile square. Except for it no other effort has been made either by Cubans or Americans to designate the lines that once encircled and menaced Santiago, and Nature, always at her best under a tropical sun, has done all in her power to disguise and forever obliterate the scene of the army's one battle. Those features which still remain unchanged are very few. The Treaty Tree, now surrounded by a tall fence, is one, the blockhouse is another. The little lake in which, even when the bullets were dropping, the men used to bathe and wash their clothes, the big iron sugar kettle that gave a new name to Kettle Hill, and here and there a trench hardly deeper than a ploughed furrow, and nearly hidden by growing plants, are the few landmarks that remain.

Of the camps of Generals Chaffee, Lawton, Bates, Sumner, and Wheeler, of Colonels Leonard Wood and Theodore Roosevelt, there are but the slightest traces. The Bloody Bend, as some call it, in the San Juan River, as some call that stream, seems to have entirely disappeared. At least, it certainly was not where it should have been, and the place the hotel guides point out to unsuspecting tourists bears not the slightest physical resemblance to that ford.

In twelve years, during one of which there has been in Santiago the most severe rainfall in sixty years, the San Juan stream has carried away its banks and the trees that lined them, and the trails that should mark where the ford once crossed have so altered and so many new ones have been added, that the exact location of the once famous dressing station is now most difficult, if not impossible, to determine. To establish the sites of the old camping grounds is but little less difficult. The headquarters of General Wheeler are easy to recognise, for the reason that the place selected was in a hollow, and the most un-healthy spot along the five miles of intrenchments. It is about thirty yards from where the road turns to rise over the ridge to Santiago, and all the water from the hill pours into it as into a rain barrel.

It was here that Troop G, Third Cavalry, under Major Hardee, as it was Wheeler's escort, was forced to bivouac, and where one-third of its number came down with fever. The camp of General Sam Sum-ner was some sixty yards to the right of the headquarters of General Wheeler, on the high shoulder of the hill just above the camp of the engineers, who were on the side of the road opposite. The camps of Generals Chaffee, Lawton, Hawkins, Ludlow, and the positions and trenches taken and held by the different regiments under them one can place only relatively.

One reason for this is that before our army attacked the hills all the underbrush and small trees that might conceal the advance of our men had been cleared away by the Spaniards, leaving the hill, except for the high crest, comparatively bare. Today the hills are thick with young trees and enormous bushes. The alteration in the landscape is as marked as is the difference between ground cleared for golf and the same spot planted with corn and fruit-trees.

Of all the camps, the one that today bears the strongest evidences of its occupation is that of the Rough Riders. A part of the camp of that regiment, which was situated on the ridge some hundred feet from the Santiago road, was pitched under a clump of shade trees, and today, even after seven years, the trunks of these trees bear the names and initials of the men who camped beneath them. (Some of the names and initials on the trees are as follows: J. P. Allen; Lynch; Luke Steed; Happy Mack, Rough Riders; Russell; Ward; E. M. Lewis, C, 9th Cav.; Alex; E. K. T.; J. P. E.; W. N. D.; R. D. R.; I. W. S., 5th U. S.; J. M. B.; J. M. T., C, 9th.) These men will remember that when they took this hill they found that the fortifications beneath the trees were partly made from the foundations of an *adobe* house.

The red tiles from its roof still litter the ground. These tiles and the names cut in the bark of the trees determine absolutely the site of one-half of the camp, but the other half, where stood Tiffany's quick-firing gun and Parker's Gatling, has been almost obliterated. The tree under which Colonel Roosevelt pitched his tent I could not discover, and the trenches in which he used to sit with his officers and with the officers from the regiments of the regular army are now levelled to make a kitchen-garden. Sometimes the ex-President is said to have too generously given office and promotion to the friends he made in Cuba. These men he met in the trenches were then not necessarily his friends. Today they are not necessarily his friends. They are the men the free life of the rifle-pits enabled him to know and to understand as the settled relations of home life and peace would never have permitted.

At that time none of them guessed that the "amateur colonel," to whom they talked freely as to a comrade, would be their commander-in-chief. They did not suspect that he would become even the next Governor of New York, certainly not that in a few years he would be the President of the United States. So, they showed themselves to him frankly, unconsciously. They criticised, argued, disagreed, and he became familiar with the views, character, and worth of each, and re-membered. The seeds planted in those half-obliterated trenches have borne greater results than ever will the kitchen-garden.

The kitchen-garden is immediately on the crest of the hill, and near it a Cuban farmer has built a shack of mud and twigs and culti-vated several acres of land. On Kettle Hill there are three more such shacks, and over all the hills the new tenants have strung stout barbed-wire fences and made new trails and reared wooden gateways. It was curious to find how greatly these modern improvements confused one's recollection of the landscape, and it was interesting, also, to find how the presence on the hills of 12,000 men and the excitement of the time magnified distances and disarranged the landscape.

During the fight I walked along a portion of the Santiago road, and for many years I always have thought of that walk as extending over immense distances. It started from the top of San Juan Hill beside the blockhouse, where I had climbed to watch our artillery in action. By a mistake, the artillery had been sent there, and it remained exposed on the crest only about three minutes. During that brief moment the black powder it burned drew upon it the fire of every rifle in the Spanish line. To load his piece, each of our men was forced to crawl to it on his stomach, rise on one elbow in order to shove in the shell and lock the breech, and then, still flat on the ground, wriggle below the crest. In the three minutes three men were wounded and two killed; and the guns were withdrawn.

I also withdrew. I withdrew first. Indeed, all that happened after the first three seconds of those three minutes is hearsay, for I was in the Santiago road at the foot of the hill and retreating briskly. This road also was under a cross-fire, which made it stretch in either direction to an interminable distance. I remember a government teamster driving a Studebaker wagon filled with ammunition coming up at a gallop out of this interminable distance and seeking shelter against the base of the hill. Seated beside him was a small boy, freckled and sunburned, a stowaway from one of the transports. He was grandly happy and excited, and his only fear was that he was not "under fire." From our coign of safety, with our backs to the hill, the teamster and I assured him that, on that point, he need feel no morbid doubt. But until a bullet embedded itself in the blue board of the wagon he was not convinced. Then with his jack-knife he dug it out and shouted with pleasure. "I guess the folks will have to believe I was in a battle now," he said.

That coign of safety ceasing to be a coign of safety caused us to move on in search of another, and I came upon Sergeant Borrowe blocking the road with his dynamite gun. He and his brother and three regulars were busily correcting a hitch in its mechanism. An officer carrying an order along the line halted his sweating horse and gazed at the strange gun with professional knowledge.

"That must be the dynamite gun I have heard so much about," he shouted. Borrowe saluted and shouted assent. The officer, greatly interested, forgot his errand.

"I'd like to see you fire it once," he said eagerly. Borrowe, delighted at the chance to exhibit his toy to a professional soldier, beamed with equal eagerness.

"In just a moment, sir," he said; "this shell seems to have jammed a bit." The officer, for the first time seeing the shell stuck in the breech, hurriedly gathered up his reins. He seemed to be losing interest. With elaborate carelessness I began to edge off down the road.

"Wait," Borrowe begged; "we'll have it out in a minute."

Suddenly I heard the officer's voice raised wildly.

"What—what," he gasped, "is that man doing with that axe?"

"He's helping me to get out this shell," said Borrowe.

"Good God!" said the officer. Then he remembered his errand.

Until last year, when I again met young Borrowe gayly disporting himself at a lawn-tennis tournament at Mattapoisett, I did not know whether his brother's method of removing dynamite with an axe had been entirely successful. He said it worked all right.

At the turn of the road I found Colonel Leonard Wood and a group of Rough Riders, who were busily intrenching. At the same moment Stephen Crane came up with "Jimmy" Hare, the man who has made the Russian-Japanese War famous. Crane walked to the crest and stood there as sharply outlined as a semaphore, observing the enemy's lines, and instantly bringing upon himself and us the fire of many Mausers. With everyone else, Wood was crouched below the crest and shouted to Crane to lie down. Crane, still standing, as though to get out of earshot, moved away, and Wood again ordered him to lie down.

"You're drawing the fire on these men," Wood commanded. Although the heat—it was the 1st of July in the tropics—was terrific, Crane wore a long India rubber rain-coat and was smoking a pipe. He appeared as cool as though he were looking down from a box at a theatre. I knew that to Crane, anything that savoured of a pose was hateful, so, as I did not want to see him killed, I called, "You're not impressing any one by doing that, Crane." As I hoped he would, he instantly dropped to his knees. When he crawled over to where we lay, I explained, "I knew that would fetch you," and he grinned, and said, "Oh, was that it?"

A captain of the cavalry came up to Wood and asked permission to withdraw his troop from the top of the hill to a trench forty feet below the one they were in. "They can't possibly live where they are now," he explained, "and they're doing no good there, for they can't raise their heads to fire. In that lower trench they would be out of range themselves and would be able to fire back."

"Yes," said Wood, "but all the other men in the first trench would see them withdraw, and the moral effect would be bad. They needn't attempt to return the enemy's fire, but they must not retreat."

The officer looked as though he would like to argue. He was a West Point graduate and a full-fledged captain in the regular army. To him, Wood, in spite of his volunteer rank of colonel, which that day, owing to the illness of General Young, had placed him in command of a brigade, was still a doctor. But discipline was strong in him, and though he looked many things, he rose from his knees and grimly saluted. But at that moment, without waiting for the permission of any one, the men leaped out of the trench and ran. It looked as though they were going to run all the way to the sea, and the sight was sickening. But they had no intention of running to the sea. They ran only to the trench forty feet farther down and jumped into it, and instantly turning, began pumping lead at the enemy.

Since five that morning Wood had been running about on his feet, his clothes stuck to him with sweat and the mud and water of forded streams, and as he rose, he limped slightly. "My, but I'm tired!" he said, in a tone of the most acute surprise, and as though that fact was the only one that was weighing on his mind. He limped over to the trench in which the men were now busily firing off their rifles and waved a riding-crop he carried at the trench they had abandoned. He was standing as Crane had been standing, in silhouette against the skyline.

"Come back, boys," we heard him shouting. "The other men can't withdraw, and so you mustn't. It looks bad. Come on, get out of that!"

What made it more amusing was that, although Wood had, like everyone else, discarded his coat and wore a strange uniform of grey shirt, white riding-breeches, and a cowboy Stetson, with no insignia of rank, not even straps pinned to his shirt, still the men instantly accepted his authority. They looked at him on the crest of the hill, waving his stick persuasively at the grave-like trench at his feet, and then with a shout scampered back to it.

After that, as I had a bad attack of sciatica and no place to sleep and nothing to eat, I accepted Crane's offer of a blanket and coffee at his bivouac near El Poso. On account of the sciatica I was not able to walk fast, and, although for over a mile of the way the trail was under fire, Crane and Hare each insisted on giving me an arm, and kept step with my stumblings. Whenever I protested and refused their sacrifice and pointed out the risk they were taking they smiled as at the ravings of a naughty child, and when I lay down in the road and refused to budge unless they left me, Crane called the attention of Hare to the effect of the setting sun behind the palm-trees. To the reader all these little things that one remembers seem very little indeed, but they were vivid at the moment, and I have always thought of them as stretching over a long extent of time and territory.

Before I revisited San Juan, I would have said that the distance along the road from the point where I left the artillery to where I joined Wood was three-quarters of a mile. When I paced it later, I found the distance was about seventy-five yards. I do not urge my stupidity or my extreme terror as a proof that others would be as greatly confused, but, if only for the sake of the stupid ones, it seems a pity that the landmarks of San Juan should not be rescued from the jungle, and a few sign-posts placed upon the hills. It is true that the great battles of the Civil War and those of the one in Manchuria, where the men killed and wounded in a day outnumber all those who fought on both sides at San Juan, make that battle read like a skirmish.

But the Spanish War had its results. At least it made Cuba into a re-public, and so enriched or burdened us with colonies that our republic

Rough Riders in the trenches

The same spot as it appears to-day

The figure in the picture is standing in what remains of the trench

changed into something like an empire. But I do not urge that. It will never be because San Juan changed our foreign policy that people will visit the spot, and will send from it picture postal cards. The human interest alone will keep San Juan alive. The men who fought there came from every State in our country and from every class of our social life. We sent there the best of our regular army, and with them, cowboys, clerks, bricklayers, football players, three future commanders of the greater army that followed that war, the future Governor of Cuba, future commanders of the Philippines, the commander of our forces in China, a future President of the United States. And, whether these men, when they returned to their homes again, became clerks and millionaires and dentists, or rose to be presidents and mounted policemen, they all remember very kindly the days they lay huddled together in the trenches on that hot and glaring sky-line.

And there must be many more besides who hold the place in memory. There are few in the United States so poor in relatives and friends who did not in his or her heart send a substitute to Cuba. For these it seems as though San Juan might be better preserved, not as it is, for already its aspect is too far changed to wish for that, but as it was. The efforts already made to keep the place in memory and to honour the Americans who died there are the public park which I have mentioned, the monument on San Juan, and one other monument at Guasimas to the regulars and Rough Riders who were killed there. To these monuments the Society of Santiago will add four more, which will mark the landing place of the army at Daiquairi and the fights at Guasimas, El Caney, and San Juan Hill.

But I believe even more than this might be done to preserve to the place its proper values. These values are sentimental, historical, and possibly to the military student, educational. If today there were erected at Daiquairi, Siboney, Guasimas, El Poso, El Caney, and on and about San Juan a dozen iron or bronze tablets that would tell from where certain regiments advanced, what posts they held, how many or how few were the men who held those positions, how near they were to the trenches of the enemy, and by whom these men were commanded, I am sure the place would reconstruct itself and would breathe with interest, not only for the returning volunteer, but for any casual tourist.

As it is, the history of the fight and the reputation of the men who fought is now at the mercy of the caretaker of the park and the Cuban "guides" from the hotel. The caretaker speaks only Spanish, and, considering the amount of misinformation the guides disseminate, it is a pity when they are talking to Americans, they are not forced to use the same language. When last I visited it, Carlos Portuondo was the official guardian of San Juan Hill. He is an aged Cuban, and he fought through the Ten Years' War, but during the last insurrection and the Spanish-American War he not only was not near San Juan, but was not even on the Island of Cuba. He is a charming old person, and so is his aged wife.

Their chief concern in life, when I saw them, was to sell me a pair of breeches made of palm-fibre which Carlos had worn throughout the entire ten years of battle. The vicissitudes of those trousers he recited to me in great detail, and he very properly regarded them as of historic value. But of what happened at San Juan he knew nothing, and when I asked him why he held his present post and occupied the Blockhouse, he said, "To keep the cows out of the park." When I asked him where the Americans had camped, he pointed carefully from the back door of the Blockhouse to the foot of his kitchen-garden. I assured him that under no stress of terror could the entire American Army have been driven into his back yard, and pointed out where it had stretched along the ridge of hills for five miles.

He politely but unmistakably showed that he thought I was a liar. From the Venus Hotel there were two guides, old Casanova and Jean Casanova, his languid and good-natured son, a youth of sixteen years. Old Casanova, like most Cubans, is not inclined to give much credit for what they did in Cuba to the Americans. After all, he says, they came only just as the Cubans themselves were about to conquer the Spaniards, and by a lucky chance received the surrender and then claimed all the credit. As other Cubans told me, "Had the Americans left us alone a few weeks longer, we would have ended the war."

How they were to have taken Havana, and sunk Cervera's fleet, and why they were not among those present when our men charged San Juan, I did not inquire. Old Casanova, again like other Cubans, ranks the fighting qualities of the Spaniard much higher than those of the American. This is only human. It must be annoying to a Cuban to remember that after he had for three years fought the Spaniard, the Yankee in eight weeks received his surrender and began to ship him home. The way Casanova describes the fight at El Caney is as follows:

The Americans thought they could capture El Caney in one day, but the brave General Toral fought so good that it was six days before the Americans could make the Spaniards surrender.

The statement is correct except as regards the length of time during which the fight lasted. The Americans did make the mistake of thinking they could eat up El Caney in an hour and then march through it to San Juan. Owing to the splendid courage of Toral and his few troops our soldiers, under two of our best generals, were held in check from seven in the morning until two in the afternoon. But the difference between seven hours of one day and six days is considerable. Still, at present at San Juan that is the sort of information upon which the patriotic and puzzled American tourist is fed.

Young Casanova, the only other authority in Santiago, is not so sure of his facts as is his father, and is willing to learn. He went with me to hold my pony while I took the photographs that accompany this article, and I listened with great interest to his accounts of the battle. Finally, he made a statement that was correct. "How did you happen to get that right?" I asked.

"Yesterday," he said, "I guided Colonel Hayes here, and while I guided him, he explained it to me."

Letters from Spanish-American War

When the news reached Richard that the Spanish-American War seemed inevitable, he returned at once to New York. Here he spent a few days in arranging to act as correspondent for the New York *Herald*, the *London Times*, and *Scribner's Magazine*, and then started for Key West.

Off Key West—April 24th, 1898.
On Board *Smith*, *Herald* Yacht.

Dear Mother:

I wrote you such a cross gloomy letter that I must drop you another to make up for it. Since I wrote that an hour ago, we have received word that war is declared and I am now on board the *Smith*. She is a really fine vessel as big as Benedict's yacht with plenty of deck room and big bunks. I have everything I want on board and *The Herald* men are two old Press men so we are good friends. If I had had another hour, I believe I could have got a berth on the flag ship for Roosevelt telegraphed me the longest and strongest letter on the subject a man could write instructing the admiral to take me on as I was writing history. Chadwick seemed willing but then the signal to set sail came and we had to stampede. All the ships have their sailing pennants up. It is as calm as a mirror thank goodness but as hot as hell.

We expect to be off Havana tomorrow at sunset. Then what we do no one knows. The crew is on strike above and the mate is wrestling with them but as it seems to be only a question of a few dollars it will come out all right. We expect to be back here on Sunday but may stay out later. Don't worry if you don't hear. It is grand to see the line of battleships five miles out like dogs in a leash puffing and straining. Thank God they'll let them slip any minute now. I don't know where "Stenie" is. I am now going to take a nap while the smooth water lasts.

Dick.

Dear Family:

I left Key West on the morning of the 24th in the *Dolphin* with the idea of trying to get on board the flagship on the strength of Roosevelt's letter. Stenie Bonsal got on just before she sailed, not as a correspondent, but as a magazine-writer for *McClure's,* who have given him a commission, and because he could act as interpreter. I left the flagship the morning of the day I arrived. The captain of the *Dolphin* apologised to his officers while we were at anchor in the harbour of Key West, because his was a "cabin" and not a "gun" ship, and because he had to deliver the mails at once on board the flagship and not turn out of his course for anything, no matter how tempting a prize it might appear to be. He then proceeded to chase every sail and column of smoke on the horizon, so that the course was like a cat's cradle.

We first headed for a big steamer and sounded "general quarters." It was fine to see the faces of the apprentices as they ran to get their cutlasses and revolvers, their eyes open and their hair on end, with the hope that they were to board a Spanish battleship. But at the first gun she ran up an American flag, and on getting nearer we saw she was a Mallory steamer. An hour later we chased another steamer, but she was already a prize, with a prize crew on board. Then we had a chase for three hours at night; after what we believed was the *Panama,* but she ran away from us. We fired three shells after her, and she still ran and got away. The next morning, I went on board the *New York* with Zogbaum, the artist. Admiral Sampson is a fine man; he impressed me very much. He was very much bothered at the order forbidding correspondents on the ship, but I talked like a father to him, and he finally gave in, and was very nice about the way he did it.

Since then I have had the most interesting time and the most novel experience of my life. We have been lying from three to ten miles off shore. We can see Morro Castle and houses and palms plainly without a glass, and with one we can distinguish men and women in the villages. It is, or was, frightfully hot, and you had to keep moving all the time to get out of the sun. I mess with the officers, but the other correspondents, the Associated Press and Ralph Paine of *The World* and *Press* of Philadelphia, with the middies. Paine got on because Scovel of *The World* has done so much secret service work for the admiral, running in at night and taking soundings, and by day making photographs of the coast, also carrying messages to the insurgents.

It is a wonderful ship, like a village, and as big as the *Paris*. We drift around in the sun or the moonlight, and when we see a light, chase after it. There is a band on board that plays twice a day. It is like a luxurious yacht, with none of the *ennui* of a yacht. The other night, when we were heading off a steamer and firing six-pounders across her bows, the band was playing the "star" song from the *Meistersinger*. Wagner and War struck me as the most *fin de siècle* idea of war that I had ever heard of. The nights have been perfectly beautiful, full of moonlight, when we sit on deck and smoke. It is like looking down from the roof of a high building. Yesterday they brought a Spanish officer on board, he had been picked up in a schooner with his orderly.

I was in Captain Chadwick's cabin when he was brought in, and Scovel interpreted for the captain, who was more courteous than any Spanish Don that breathes. The officer said he had been on his way to see his wife and newly born baby at Matanzas, and had no knowledge that war had been declared. I must say it did me good to see him. I remembered the way the Spanish officers used to insult me in a language which I, fortunately for me, could not understand, and how I hated the sight of them, and I enjoyed seeing his red and yellow cockade on the table before me, while I sat in a big armchair and smoked and was in hearing of the marines drilling on the upper deck. He was invited to go to breakfast with the officers, and I sat next to him, and as it happened to be my turn to treat, I had the satisfaction of pouring drinks down his throat.

I told stories about Spanish officers all the time to the rest of the mess, pretending I was telling them something else by making drawings on the tablecloth, so that the unhappy officer on his other side, who was talking Spanish to him, had a hard time not to laugh. I told Zogbaum he ought to draw a picture of him at the mess to show how we treated prisoners, and a companion one of the captain of the *Compeliton*, who came over with us on the *Dolphin*, and who showed us the marks of the ropes on his wrists and arms the Spaniards had bound him with when he was in Cabanas for nine months. The orderly messed with the bluejackets, who treated him in the most hospitable manner. He was a poor little peasant boy, half-starved and hollow-eyed, and so scared that he could hardly stand, but they took great pride in the fact that they had made him eat three times of everything. They are, without prejudice, the finest body of men and boys you would care to see, and as humorous and polite and keen as any class of men I ever met.

The war could be ended in a month so far as the island of Cuba is concerned, if the troops were ready and brought over here. The coast to Havana for ten miles is broad enough for them to march along it, and the heights above could be covered the entire time by the fleet, so that it would be absolutely impossible for any force to withstand the awful hailstorm they would play on it. Transports carrying the provisions would be protected by the ships on the gulf side, and the guns at Morro could be shut up in twenty-four hours. This is not a dream, but the most obvious and feasible plan, and it is a disgrace if the Washington politicians delay.

As to health, this is the healthiest part of the coast. The trade winds blow every day of the year, and the fever talk is all nonsense. The army certainly has delayed most scandalously in mobilizing. This talk of waiting a month is suicide. It is a terrible expense. It keeps the people on a strain, destroys business, and the health of the troops at Tampa is, to my mind, in much greater danger than it would be on the hills around Havana, where, as Scovel says, there is as much yellow fever as there is snow. Tell Dad to urge them to act promptly. In the meanwhile, I am having a magnificent time. I am burned and hungry and losing about a ton of fat a day, and I sleep finely. The other night the Porter held us up, but it was a story that never got into the papers. I haven't missed a trick so far except not getting on the flagship from the first, but that does not count now since I am on board.

I haven't written anything yet, but I am going to begin soon. I expect to make myself rich on this campaign. I get ten cents a word from *Scribner's* for everything I send them, if it is only a thousand words, and I get four hundred dollars a week salary from *The Times*, and all my expenses. I haven't had any yet, but when I go back and join the army, I am going to travel *en suite* with an assistant and the best and gentlest ponies; a courier and a servant, a tent and a secretary and a typewriter, so that Miles will look like a second lieutenant.

When I came out here on the *Dolphin,* I said I was going to Tampa, lying just on the principle that it is no other newspaper-man's business where you are going. So, *The Herald* man at Key West, hearing this, and *not knowing I was going to the flagship*, called Long, making a strong kick about the correspondents, Bonsal, Remington and Paine, who are, or were, with the squadron. Stenie left two days ago, hoping to get a commission on the staff of General Lee. So yesterday Scovel told me Long had cabled in answer to *The Herald's* protests to the admiral as follows:

> Complaints have been received that correspondents Paine, Remington and Bonsal are with the squadron. Send them ashore at once. There must be no favouritism.

Scovel got the admiral at once to cable Long on his behalf because of his services as a spy, but as Roosevelt had done so much for me, I would not appeal over him, and this morning I sent in word to the admiral that I was leaving the ship and would like to pay my respects. Sampson is a thin man with a grey beard. He looks like a college professor and has very fine, gentle eyes. He asked me why I meant to leave the ship, and I said I had heard one of the torpedo boats was going to Key West, and I thought I would go with her if he would allow it. He asked if I had seen the cable from Long, and I said I had heard of it, and that I was really going so as not to embarrass him with my presence. He said:

> I have received three different orders from the secretary, one of them telling me I could have such correspondents on board as were agreeable to me. He now tells me that they must all go. You can do as you wish. You are perfectly welcome to remain until the conflict of orders is cleared up.

I saw he was mad and that he wanted me to stay, or at least not to go of my own wish, so that he could have a grievance out of it—if he had to send me away after having been told he could have those with him who were agreeable to him. Captain Chadwick was in the cabin, and said, "Perhaps Mr. Davis had better remain another twenty-four hours."

The admiral added, "Ships are going to Key West daily." Then Chadwick repeated that he thought I had better stay another day, and made a motion to me to do so. So, I said I would, and now I am waiting to see what is going to happen. Outside, Chadwick told me that something in the way of an experience would probably come off, so I have hopes. By this time, of course, you know all about it. I shall finish this later.

We began bombarding Matanzas twenty minutes after I wrote the above. It was great. I guess I got a beat, as *The Herald* tug is the only one in sight.

Dick.

Flagship—Off Havana
April 30th, 1898.

Dear Family:

You must not mind if I don't write often, but I feel that you see *The Herald* every day and that tells you of what I am seeing and doing, and I am writing so much, and what with keeping notes and all, I haven't much time—What you probably want to know is that I am well and that my sciatica is not troubling me at all—Mother always wants to know that. On the other hand I am on the best ship from which to see things and on the safest, as she can move quicker and is more heavily armoured than any save the battleships—The fact that the admiral is on board and that she is the flagship is also a guarantee that she will not be allowed to expose herself. I was very badly scared when I first came to Key West for fear I should be left especially when I didn't make the flagship—But I have not missed a single trick so far—Bonsal missed the bombardment and so did Stephen Crane—All the press boats were away except *The Herald's.* I had to write the story in fifteen minutes, so it was no good except that we had it exclusively—

I am sending a short story of the first shot fired to the Scribner's and am arranging with them to bring out a book on the campaign. I have asked them to announce it as it will help me immensely here for it is as an historian and not as a correspondent that I get on over those men who are correspondents for papers only. I have made I think my position here very strong and the admiral is very much my friend as are also his staff. Crane on the other hand took the place of Paine who was exceedingly popular with everyone and it has made it hard for Crane to get into things—I am having a really royal time, it is so beautiful by both night and day and there is always colour and movement and the most rigid discipline with the most hearty good feeling—I get on very well with the crew too, one of them got shot by a revolver's going off and I asked the surgeon if I might not help at the operation so that I might learn to be useful, and to get accustomed to the sight of wounds and surgery.

It was a wonderful thing to see, and I was confused as to whether I admired the human body more or the way the surgeon's understood and mastered it—The sailor would not give way to the ether and I had to hold him for an hour while they took out his whole insides and laid them on the table and felt around inside of him as though he were a hollow watermelon. Then they put his stomach back and sewed it in and then sewed up his skin and he was just as good as new.

We carried him over to a cot and he came to, and looked up at us. We were all bare-armed and covered with his blood, and then over at the operating table, which was also covered with his blood. He was grey under his tan and his lips were purple and his eyes were still drunk with the ether—But he looked at our sanguinary hands and shook his head sideways on the pillow and smiled—"You'se can't kill me," he said, "I'm a *New Yorker*, by God—you'se can't kill me."

The *Herald* cabled for a story as to how the crew of the *New York* behaved in action. I think I shall send them that although there are a few things the people had better take for granted—Of course, we haven't been "in action" yet but the first bombardment made me nervous until it got well started. I think everyone was rather nervous and it was chiefly to show them there was nothing to worry about that we fired off the U. S. guns. They talk like veterans now—It was much less of a strain than I had expected, there was no standing on your toes nor keeping your mouth open or putting wadding in your ears.

I took photographs most of the time, and they ought to be excellent—what happened was that you were thrown up off the deck just as you are when an elevator starts with a sharp jerk and there was an awful noise like the worst clap of thunder you ever heard close to your ears, then the smoke covered everything and you could hear the shot going through the air like a giant rocket—The shots they fired at us did not cut any ice except a shrapnel that broke just over the main mast and which reminded me of Greece—The other shots fell short—The best thing was to see the captains of the *Puritan* and *Cincinnati* frantically signalling to be allowed to fire too—A little fort had opened on us from the left so they plugged at that, it was a wonderful sight, the *Monitor* was swept with waves and the guns seemed to come out of the water.

The *Cincinnati* did the best of all. Her guns were as fast as the reports of a revolver, a self-cocking revolver, when one holds the trigger for the whole six. We got some copies of *The Lucha* on the *Panama* and their accounts of what was going on in Havana were the best reading I ever saw—They probably reported the Matanzas bombardment as a Spanish victory—The firing yesterday was very tame. We all sat about on deck and the band played all the time—We didn't even send the men to quarters—I do not believe the army intends to move for two weeks yet, so I shall stay here. They seem to want me to do so, and I certainly want to—But that army is too slow for words, and we love the "Notes from the Front" in *The Tribune*, telling about the troops at

Chickamauga—I believe what will happen is that a chance shot will kill some of our men, and the admiral won't do a thing but knock hell out of whatever fort does it and land a party of marines and bluejackets—Even if they only occupy the place for 24 hours, it will beat that army out and that's what I want.

They'll get second money in the campaign if they get any, unless they brace up and come over—I have the very luck of the British Army, I walked into an open hatch today and didn't stop until I caught by my arms and the back of my neck. It was very dark and they had opened it while I was in a cabin. The Jackie whose business it was to watch it was worse scared than I was, and I looked up at him while still hanging to the edges with my neck and arms and said "why didn't you tell me?"

He shook his head and said, "that's so, Sir, I certainly should have told you, I certainly should"—They're exactly like children and the reason is, I think, because they are so shut off from the contamination of the world. One of these ships is like living in a monastery, and they are as disciplined and gentle as monks, and as reckless as cowboys. When I go forward and speak to one of them they all gather round and sit on the deck in circles and we talk and they listen and make the most interesting comments.

The middy who fired the first gun at Matanzas is a modest alert boy about 18 years old and crazy about his work—So, the captain selected him for the honour and also because there is such jealousy between the bow and stern guns that he decided not to risk feelings being hurt by giving it to either—So, Boone who was at Annapolis a month ago was told to fire the shot—We all took his name and he has grown about three inches.

We told him all of the United States and England would be ringing with his name—When I was alone he came and sat down on a gull beside me and told me he was very glad they had let him fire that first gun because his mother was an invalid and he had gone into the navy against her wish and he hoped now that she would be satisfied when she saw his name in the papers. He was too sweet and boyish about it for words and I am going to take a snapshot at him and put his picture in *Scribner's*—"he only stands about so high—"

Dick.

I enclose a souvenir of the bombardment. Please keep it carefully for me—It was the first shot "in anger" in thirty years.

Tampa, May 3rd, 1898.

Dear Nora:

We are still here and probably will be. It is a merry war, if there were only some girls here the place would be perfect. I don't know what's the matter with the American girl—here am I—and Stenie and Willie Chanler and Frederick Remington and all the boy officers of the army and not one solitary, ugly, plain, pretty, or beautiful girl. I bought a fine pony today, her name was Ellaline but I thought that was too much glory for Ellaline so I diffused it over the whole company by re-christening her Gaiety Girl, because she is so quiet, all the Gaiety Girls I know are quiet. She never does what I tell her anyway, so it doesn't matter what I call her. But when this cruel war is over ($6 a day with bath room adjoining) I am going to have an oil painting of her labelled "Gaiety Girl the Kentucky Mare that carried the news of the fall of Havana to Matanzas, fifty miles under fire and Richard Harding Davis."

Tomorrow I am going to buy a saddle and a servant. War is a cruel thing especially to army officers. They have to wear uniforms and are not allowed to take off their trousers to keep cool—They take off everything else except their hats and sit in the dining room without their coats or collars—That's because it is war time.

They are terrible brave—you can see it by the way they wear bouquets on their tunics and cigarette badges and Cuban flags and by not saluting their officers.

One general counted today and forty enlisted men passed him without saluting. The army will have to do a lot of fighting to make itself solid with me. They are mounted police. We have a sentry here, he sits in a rocking chair. Imagine one of Sampson's or Dewey's blue-jackets sitting down even on a gun carriage. Wait till I write my book. I wouldn't say a word now but when I write that book, I'll give them large space rates. I am writing it now, the first batch comes out in *Scribner's* in July.

Love to you all.   Dick.

★★★★★★

During the early days of the war, Richard received the appointment of a captaincy, but on the advice of his friends that his services were more valuable as a correspondent, he refused the commission. The following letter shows that at least at the time my brother regretted the decision, but as events turned out he succeeded in rendering splendid service not only as a correspondent but in the field.

Tampa—May 14, 1898.

Dear Chas.

On reflection I am greatly troubled that I declined the captaincy. It is unfortunate that I had not time to consider it. We shall not have another war and I can always be a war correspondent in other countries but never again have a chance to serve in my own. The people here think it was the right thing to do but the outside people won't. Not that I care about that, but I think I was weak not to chance it. I don't know exactly what I ought to do. When I see all these kid militia men enlisted it makes me feel like the devil. I've no doubt many of them look upon it as a sort of a holiday and an outing and like it for the excitement, but it would bore me to death. The whole thing would bore me if I thought I had to keep at it for a year or more. That is the fault of my having had too much excitement and freedom. It spoils me to make sacrifices that other men can make.

Whichever way it comes out I shall be sorry and feel I did not do the right thing. Lying around this hotel is enough to demoralise anybody. We are much more out of it than you are, and one gets cynical and loses interest. On the other hand, I would be miserable to go back and have done nothing. It is a question of character entirely and I don't feel I've played the part at all. It's all very well to say you are doing more by writing, but are you? It's an easy game to look on and pat the other chaps on the back with a few paragraphs, that is cheap patriotism. They're taking chances and you're not and when the war's over they'll be happy and I won't. The man that enlists or volunteers even if he doesn't get further than Chickamauga or Gretna Green and the man who doesn't enlist at all but minds his own business is much better off than I will be writing about what other men do and not doing it myself, especially as I had a chance of a life time, and declined it. I'll always feel I lost in character by not sticking to it whether I had to go to Arizona or Governor's Island.

I was unfortunate in having Lee and Remington to advise me. We talked for two hours in Fred's bedroom and they were both dead against it and Lee composed my telegram to the president. Now, I feel sure I did wrong. Shafter did not care and the other officers were delighted and said it was very honourable and manly giving me credit for motives I didn't have. I just didn't think it was good enough although I wanted it too and I missed something I can never get again.

140

I am very sad about it. I know all the arguments for not taking it but as a matter of fact I should have done so. I would have made a good *aide*, and had I got a chance I certainly would have won out and been promoted. That there are fools appointed with me is no answer. I wouldn't have stayed in their class long.

Dick.

Tampa, May 29, 1898.

Dear Chas.:

The cigars came; they are O. K. and a great treat after Tampa products. Captain Lee and I went out to the volunteer camps today: Florida, Alabama, Ohio and Michigan, General Lee's push, and it has depressed me very much. I have been so right about so many things these last five years, and was laughed at for making much of them. Now all I urged is proved to be correct; nothing our men wear is right. The shoes, the hats, the coats, all are dangerous to health and comfort; one-third of the men cannot wear the regulation shoe because it cuts the instep, and buy their own, and the volunteers are like the Cuban Army in appearance. The Greek Army, at which I made such sport, is a fine organisation in comparison as far as outfit goes; of course, there is no comparison in the spirit of the men. One colonel of the Florida regiment told us that one-third of his men had never fired a gun. They live on the ground; there are no rain trenches around the tents, or gutters along the company streets; the latrines are dug to *windward* of the camp, and all the refuse is burned to windward.

Half of the men have no uniforms nor shoes. I pointed out some of the unnecessary discomforts the men were undergoing through ignorance, and one colonel, a Michigan politician, said, "Oh, well, they'll learn. It will be a good lesson for them." Instead of telling them, or telling their captains, he thinks it best that they should find things out by suffering. I cannot decide whether to write anything about it or not. I cannot see where it could do any good, for it is the system that is wrong—the whole volunteer system, I mean. Captain Lee happened to be in Washington when the first Manila outfit was starting from San Francisco, and it was on his representations that they gave the men hammocks, and took a store of Mexican dollars. They did not know that Mexican dollars are the only currency of the East, and were expecting to pay the men in drafts on New York.

Isn't that a pitiable situation when a captain of an English company happens to stray into the war office, and happens to have a good heart and busies himself to see that our own men are supplied with hammocks and spending money. None of our officers had ever seen khaki until they saw Lee's, nor a cork helmet until they saw mine and his; now, naturally, they won't have anything else, and there is not another one in the country. The helmets our troops wear would be smashed in one tropical storm, and they are so light that the sun beats through them. They are also a glaring white, and are cheap and nasty and made of pasteboard. The felt hats are just as bad; the brim is not broad enough to protect them from the sun or to keep the rain off their necks, and they are made of such cheap cotton stuff that they grow hard when they are wet and heavy, instead of shedding the rain as good felt would do. They have always urged that our uniforms, though not smart nor "for show," were for use. The truth is, as they all admit, that for the tropics they are worse than useless, and that in any climate they are cheap and poor.

I could go on for pages, but it has to be written later; now they would only think it was an attack on the army. But it is sickening to see men being sacrificed as these men will be. This is the worst season of all in the Philippines. The season of typhoons and rainstorms and hurricanes, and they would have sent the men off without anything to sleep on but the wet ground and a wet blanket. It has been a great lesson for me, and I have rubber tents, rubber blankets, rubber coats and hammocks enough for an army corps. I have written nothing for the paper, because, if I started to tell the truth at all, it would do no good, and it would open up a hell of an outcry from all the families of the boys who have volunteered. Of course, the only answer is a standing army of a hundred thousand, and no more calling on the patriotism of men unfitted and untrained. It is the sacrifice of the innocents.

The incompetence and, unreadiness of the French in 1870 was no worse than our own is now. It is a terrible and pathetic spectacle, and the readiness of the volunteers to be sacrificed is all the more pathetic. It seems almost providential that we had this false-alarm call with Spain to show the people how utterly helpless they are.

love,   Dick.

Tampa, June 9th, 1898.

Well, here we are again. Talk of the "Retreat from Ottawa" I've retreated more in this war than the Greeks did. If they don't brace up soon, I'll go North and refuse to "recognise" the war. I feel I deserve a pension and a medal as it is. We had everything on board and our cabins assigned us and our "war kits" in which we set forth taken off, and were in yachting flannels ready for the five days cruise. I had the devil of a time getting out to the flagship, as they call the headquarters boat. I went out early in the morning of the night when I last wrote you. I stayed up all that night watching troops arrive and lending a helping hand and a word of cheer to dispirited mules and men, also segars and cool drinks, none of them had had food for twenty-four hours and the yellow Florida people having robbed them all day had shut up and wouldn't open their miserable shops. They even put sentries over the drinking water of the express company which is only making about a million a day out of the soldiers.

So, their soldiers slept along the platform and trucks rolled by them all night, shaking the boards on which they lay by an inch or two. About four we heard that Shafter was coming and an officer arrived to have his luggage placed on the *Seguranca*. I left them all on the pier carrying their own baggage and sweating and dripping and no one having slept. Their special train had been three hours in coming nine miles. I hired a small boat and went off to the flagship alone but the small boat began to leak and I bailed and the coloured boy pulled and the men on the transports cheered us on.

Just at the sinking point I hailed a catboat and we transferred the admiral's flag to her and also my luggage. The rest of the day we spent on the transport. We left it this morning. Some are still on it but as they are unloading all the horses and mules from the other transports fifteen having died from the heat below deck and as they cannot put them on again under a day, I am up here to get cool and to stretch my legs. The transport is all right if it were not so awfully crowded. I am glad I held out to go with the Headquarter staff. I would have died on the regular press boat, as it is the men are interesting on our boat. We have all the military attaches and Lee, Remington, Whitney and Bonsal.

The reason we did not go was because last night the *Eagle* and *Resolute* saw two Spanish cruisers and two torpedo boats laying for us outside, only five miles away. What they need with fourteen ships of war to guard a bottled up fleet and by leaving twenty-six transports some of them with 1,400 men on them without any protection but a small cruiser and one gun boat is beyond me. The whole thing is beyond me. It is the most awful picnic that ever happened, you wouldn't credit the mistakes that are made. It is worse than the French at Sedan a million times. We are just amateurs at war and about like the Indians Columbus discovered. I am exceedingly pleased with myself at taking it so good naturedly. I would have thought I would have gone mad or gone home long ago.

Bonsal and Remington threaten to go every minute. Miles tells me we shall have to wait until those cruisers are located or bottled up. I'm tired of bottling up fleets. I like the way Dewey bottles them. What a story that would have made. Twenty-six transports with as many thousand men sunk five miles out and two-thirds of them drowned. Remember the *Maine* indeed! they'd better remember the *Maine* and brace up. If we wait until they catch those boats I may be here for another month as we cannot dare go away for long or far. If we decide to go with a convoy which is what we ought to do, we may start in a day or two. Nothing you read in the papers is correct.

Did I tell you that Miles sent Dorst after me the other night and made me a long speech, saying he thought I had done so well in refusing the commission. I was glad he felt that way about it. Well, lots of love. I'm now going to take a bath. God bless you, this is a "merry war."

Richard.

In sight of Santiago—
June 26th, 1898.

Dear Chas.

We have come to a halt here in a camp along the trail to Santiago. You can see it by climbing a hill. Instead of which I am now sitting by a fine stream on a cool rock. I have discovered that you really enjoy things more when you are not getting many comforts than you do when you have all you want. That sounds dull but it is most consoling. I had a bath this morning in these rocks that I would not have given up for all the good dinners I ever had at the Waldorf, or the Savoy. It just went up and down my spine and sent thrills all over me. It is most interesting now and all the troubles of the dull days of waiting at Tampa and that awful time on the troopship are over. The army is stretched out along the trail from the coast for six miles.

Santiago lies about five miles ahead of us. I am very happy and content and the book for Scribners ought to be an interesting one. It is really very hard that my despatches are limited to 100 words for there are lots of chances. The fault lies with the army people at Washington, who give credentials to anyone who asks. To *The Independent* and other periodicals—in no sense newspapers, and they give seven to one paper, consequently we as a class are a pest to the officers and to each other. Fortunately, the survival of the fittest is the test and only the best men in every sense get to the front. There are fifty others at the base who keep the wire loaded with remorse, so when after great difficulty we get the correct news back to Daiquiri a Siboney there is no room for it.

Some of the "war correspondents" have absolutely nothing but the clothes they stand in, and the others had to take up subscriptions for them. They gambled all the time on the transports and are ensconced now at the base with cards and counters and nothing else. Whitney has turned out great at the work and I am glad he is not on a daily paper or he would share everything with me. John Fox, Whitney and I are living on Wood's Rough Riders. We are very welcome and Roosevelt has us at Headquarters but, of course, we see the men we know all the time. You get more news with the other regiments but the officers, even the generals, are such narrow-minded slipshod men that we only visit them to pick up information.

Whitney and I were the only correspondents that saw the fight at Guasimas. He was with the regulars but I had the luck to be with Roosevelt. He is sore but still he saw more than anyone else and is proportionally happy. Still he naturally would have liked to have been with our push. We were within thirty yards of the Spaniards and his crowd were not nearer than a quarter of a mile which was near enough as they had nearly as many killed. Gen. Chaffee told me today that it was Wood's charge that won the day, without it the tenth could not have driven the Spaniards back—Wood is a great young man, he has only one idea or rather all his ideas run in one direction, his regiment, he eats and talks nothing else. He never sleeps more than four hours and all the rest of the time he is moving about among the tents—Between you and me and the policeman, it was a very hot time—Maybe if I drew you a map you would understand why.

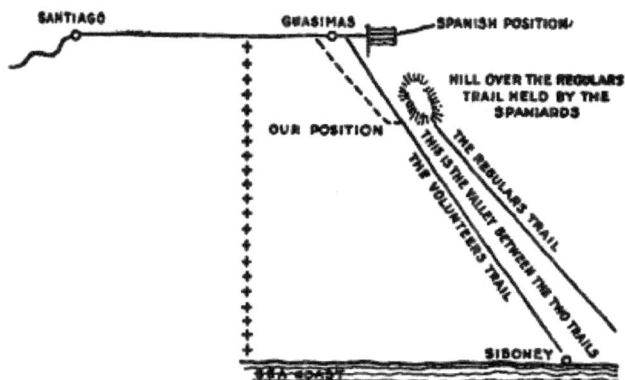

Wood and Gen. Young, by agreement the night before and without orders from anybody decided to advance at daybreak and dislodge the Spaniards from Las Guasimas. They went by two narrow trails single file, the two trails were along the crests of a line of hills with a valley between. The dotted line is the trail we should have taken had the Cubans told us it existed, if we had done so we would have had the Spaniards in the front-band rear as General Young would have caught them where they expected him to come, and we would have caught them where they were not looking for us. Of course, the Cubans who are worthless in every way never told us of this trail until we had had the meeting.

No one knew we were near Spaniards until both columns were on the place where the two trails meet. Then our scouts came back and reported them and the companies were scattered out as you see them in the little dots. The Spaniards were absolutely hidden not over 25 *per cent* of the men saw one of them for two hours—I ran out with the company on the right of the dotted line, marked "our position." I thought it was a false alarm and none of us believed there were any Spaniards this side of Santiago. The ground was covered with high grass and cactus and vines so that you could not see twenty feet ahead, the men had to beat the vines with their carbines to get through them. We had not run fifty yards through the jungle before they opened on us with a quick firing gun at a hundred yards. I saw the enemy on the hill across the valley and got six sharp shooters and began on them, then the fire got so hot that we had to lie on our faces and crawl back to the rear. I had a wounded man to carry and was in a very bad way because I had sciatica.

Two of his men took him off while I stopped to help a worse wounded trooper, but I found he was dead. When I had come back for him in an hour, the vultures had eaten out his eyes and lips. In the meanwhile, a trooper stood up on the crest with a guidon and waved it at the opposite trail to find out if the firing there was from Spaniards or Len Young's negroes. He was hit in three places but established the fact that Young was up on the trail on our right across the valley for they cheered. He was a man who had run on the Gold Ticket for Congress in Arizona, and consequently, as someone said, naturally should have led a forlorn hope. A black guard had just run past telling them that Wood was killed and that he had been ordered to Siboney for reinforcements. That was how the report spread that we were cut to pieces—A reporter who ran away from Young's column was responsible for the story that I was killed.

146

A consultation at General Wheeler's headquarters.
General Wheeler, General Wood, Colonel Dorst, Colonel Roosevelt, R. H. D., and others.

He meant Marshall who was on the left of the line and who was shot through the spine—There was a lot of wounded at the base and the fighting in front was fearful to hear. It was as fast as a hard football match and you must remember it lasted two full hours; during that time the men were on their feet all the time or crawling on their hands— Not one of them, with the exception of ———, and a sergeant who threw away his gun and ran, went a step back. It was like playing blindman's buff and you were it. I got separated once and was scared until I saw the line again, as my leg was very bad and I could not get about over the rough ground. I went down the trail and I found Capron dying and the whole place littered with discarded blankets and haversacks. I also found Fish and pulled him under cover—he was quite dead—Then I borrowed a carbine and joined Capron's troop, a second lieutenant and his sergeant were in command. The man next me in line got a bullet through his sleeve and one through his shirt and you could see where it went in and came out without touching the skin.

The firing was very high and we were in no danger so I told the lieutenant to let us charge across an open place and take a tin shack which was held by the Spaniards' rear-guard, for they were open in retreat. Roosevelt ordered his men to do the same thing and we ran forward cheering across the open and then dropped in the grass and fired. I guess I fired about twenty rounds and then formed into a strategy board and went off down the trail to scout. I got lonely and was coming back when I met another trooper who sat down and said he was too hot to run in any direction Spaniard or no Spaniard. So, we sat down and panted.

At last he asked me if I was R. H. D. and I said I was and he said "I'm Dean, I met you in Harvard in the racquet court." Then we embraced—the tenth came up then and it was all over. My leg, thank goodness, is all right again and has been so for three days. It was only the running about that caused it. I won't have to run again as I have a horse now and there will be no more ambushes and moreover, we have 12,000 men around us—Being together that way in a tight place has made us all friends and I guess I'll stick to the regiment. Send this to dear Mother and tell her I was not born to be killed. I ought to tell you more of the charming side of the life—we are all dirty and hungry and sleep on the ground and have grand talks on every subject around the headquarters tent. I was never more happy and content and never so well.

It is hot but at night it is quite cool and there has been no rain

148

only a few showers. No one is ill and there have been no cases of fever. I have not heard from you or any one since the 14th, which is not really long but so much goes on that it seems so.

Lots of love to you all.

Dick.

After reading this over I ought perhaps to say that the position of the real correspondents is absolutely the very best. No one confounds us with the men at the base, and nothing they have they deny us. We are treated immeasurably better than the poor *attachés* who are still on the ship and who if they were spies could not be treated worse. But for Whitney, Remington and myself nothing is too good. Generals fight to have us on their staffs and all that sort of thing, so I really cannot complain, except about the fact that our real news is crowded out by the faker in the rear.

Santiago.
Headquarters
Cavalry Division, U. S. Army.
Headqrs. Wood's Rough Riders.
June 29th, 1898.

Dear Dad

I suppose you are back from Marion now and I have missed you. I can't tell you how sorry I am. I wanted to see you coming up the street this summer in your knickerbockers and with no fish, but still happy. Never mind, we shall do the theatres this Fall, and have good walks downtown. I hope Mother will come up and visit me this September, at Marion and sit on Allen's and on the Clarks' porch and we can have Chas. too. I suppose he will have had his holiday but he can come up for a Sunday. We expect to move up on Santiago the day after tomorrow, and it's about time for the trail will not be passable much longer. It rains every day at three o'clock for an hour and such rain you never guessed. It is three inches high for an hour. Then we all go out naked and dig trenches to get it out of the way. It is very rough living.

I have to confess that I never knew how well off I was until I got to smoking Durham tobacco and I've only half a bag of that left. The enlisted men are smoking dried horse droppings, grass, roots and tea. Some of them can't sleep they are so nervous for the want of it, but today a lot came up and all will be well for them. I've had a steady ration of coffee, bacon and hard tack for a week and one mango, tonight we had beans. Of course, what they ought to serve is rice and beans as fried bacon is impossible in this heat. Still, everyone is well. This is the best crowd to be with—they are so well educated and so interesting. The regular army men are very dull and narrow and would bore one to death. We have Wood, Roosevelt, Lee, the British *Attaché*, Whitney and a Doctor Church, a friend of mine from Princeton, who is quite the most cheerful soul and the funniest I ever met. He carried four men from the firing line the other day back half a mile to the hospital tent. He spends most of his time coming around headquarters in an undershirt of mine and a gold bracelet fighting tarantulas.

I woke up the other morning with one seven inches long and as hairy as your head reposing on my pillow. My sciatica bothers me but has not prevented me seeing everything and I can dig rain gutters and cut wood with any of them. It is very funny to see Larned, the tennis champion, whose every movement at Newport was applauded by hundreds of young women, marching up and down in the wet grass. Whitney and I guy him. Today a sentry on post was reading *As You Like It* and whenever I go down the line half the men want to know who won the boat race—Today Wood sent me out with a detail on a pretence of scouting but really to give them a chance to see the country. They were all college boys, with Willie Tiffany as sergeant and we had a fine time and could see the Spanish sentries quite plainly without a glass.

I hope you will not worry over this long separation. I don't know of any experience I have had which has done me so much good, and being with such a fine lot of fellows is a great pleasure. The scenery is very beautiful when it is not raining. I have a cot raised off the ground in the colonel's tent and am very well off. If Chaffee or Lawton, who are the finest type of officers I ever saw, were in command, we would have been fighting every day and would probably have been in by this time. This weather shows that Havana must be put off after Porto Rico. They cannot campaign in this mud.

Dick.

Santiago, July 1898.

Dear Family

This is just to reassure you that I am all right. I and Marshall were the only correspondents with Roosevelt. We were caught in a clear case of ambush. Every precaution had been taken, but the natives knew the ground and our men did not. It was the hottest, nastiest fight I ever imagined. We never saw the enemy except glimpses. Our men fell all over the place, shouting to the others not to mind them, but to

With Colonel Roosevelt in Cuba.

go on. I got excited and took a carbine and charged the sugar house, which was what is called the key to the position. If the men had been regulars I would have sat in the rear as B———did, but I knew every other one of them, had played football, and all that sort of thing, with them, so I thought as an American I ought to help. The officers were falling all over the shop, and after it was all over Roosevelt made me a long speech before some of the men, and offered me a captaincy in the regiment any time I wanted it.

He told the Associated Press man that there was no officer in his regiment who had "been of more help or shown more courage" than your humble servant, so that's all right. After this I keep quiet. I promise I keep quiet.

Love to you all.   Richard.

★★★★★★★★

From Cuba Richard sailed with our forces to Porto Rico, where his experiences in the Spanish-American war came to an end, and he returned to Marion. He spent the fall in New York, and early in 1899 went to London.

One of the most interesting, certainly the most widely talked of, "sporting events" for which Richard was responsible was the sending of an English district-messenger boy from London to Chicago. The idea was inspired by my brother's general admiration of the London messenger service and his particular belief in one William Thomas Jaggers, a fourteen-year-old lad whom Richard had frequently employed to carry notes and run errands. One day, during a casual luncheon conversation at the Savoy with his friend Somers Somerset, Richard said that he believed that if Jaggers were asked to carry a message to New York that he could not only do it but would express no surprise at the commission. This conversation resulted in the bet described in the following letters. The boy slipped quietly away from London, but a few days later the bet became public and the newspapers were filled with speculation as to whether Jaggers could beat the mails.

The messenger carried three letters, one to my sister, one to Miss Cecil Clark of Chicago, whom Richard married a few months later, and one to myself. As a matter of fact, Jaggers delivered his notes several hours before letters travelling by the same boat reached the same destinations. The newspapers not only printed long accounts of Jaggers's triumphal progress from New York to Chicago and back again, but used the success of his undertaking as a text for many editorials against the dilatory methods of our foreign-mail service. Jaggers left London on March 11, 1899, and was back again on the 29th, having travelled nearly eighty-four hundred miles in eighteen days. On his return he was received literally by a crowd of thousands, and his feat was given official recognition by a gold medal pinned on his youthful chest by the Duchess of Rutland. Also, later on, at a garden fete he was presented to the queen, and incidentally, still later, returned to the United States as "buttons" to my brother's household.

Bachelors' Club,
Piccadilly, W.
March 15th, 1899.

Dear Chas.

I hope you are not annoyed about Jaggers. When he started no one knew of it but three people and I had no idea anyone else would, but the company sent it to *The Mail* without my name but describing me as "an American gentleman"—Instantly the foreign correspondents went to them to find out who I was and to whom I was sending the letter—I told the company it was none of their damned business—that I employed the boy by the week and that I could send him wherever I chose. Then the boy's father got proud and wrote to *The Mail* about his age and so they got the boy's name. Mine, however, is still out of it, but in America they are sure to know as the people on the steamer are crazy about him and Kinsey the Purser knows he is sent by me.

After he gets back from Chicago and Philadelphia, you can do with him as you like until the steamer sails. If the thing is taken up as it is here and the fat is in the fire, then you can do as you please—I mean you can tell the papers about it or not—Somerset holds one end of the bets and I the other. There are two bets: one that he will beat the mail to Chicago, Somerset agreeing to consider the letter you give him to Bruce, as equivalent to one coming from here. The other bet is that he will deliver and get receipts from you, Nora and Bruce, and return here by the 5th of April—You and Bobby ought to be able to do well by him if it becomes, as I say, so far public that there is no possibility of further concealment—You have my permission to do what you please—He is coming into my employ as soon as he gets back and as soon as the company give him a medal.

Over here there is the greatest possible interest in the matter—At the Clubs I go to, the waiters all wait on me in order to have the latest developments and when it was cabled over here that the Customs'

people intended stopping him, indignation raged at the Foreign Office.
Lots of love,   Dick.

89 Jermyn Street, S. W.
March, 1899

Dear Nora:

This is to be handed to you by my special messenger, who is to assure you that I am in the best of health and spirits—Keep him for a few hours and then send him on to Chicago—As he is doing this on a bet, do not give him any written instructions only verbal ones. I am very well and happy and send you all my love—Jaggers has been running errands for me ever since I came here, and a most loyal servitor when I was ill—On his return I want to keep him on as a buttons. See that he gets plenty to eat—If he comes back alive, he will have broken the messenger boy service record by three thousand miles. Personally, it does not cost me anything to speak of. The dramatisation of the soldiers continues briskly, and Maude is sending Grundy back the Jackal, to have a second go at it. Maude insists on its being done—so I stand to win a lot.

Richard.

Beefsteak Club,
9, Green Street,
Leicester Square, W. C. Tuesday.
March, 1899.

Dear Mother:—

The faithful Jaggers should have arrived today, or will do so this evening—I am sure you will make the poor little chap comfortable— I do regret having sent him on such a journey especially since the papers here made such an infernal row over it—However, neither of us will lose by it in the end—

I dined with Lady Clarke last night and met Lord Castleton there and he invited me up to Dublin for the Punchtown Races—I have a great mind to go and write a story on them—Castleton is a great sport and very popular at home and in England and it would be a pleasant experience. Kuhne Beveridge is doing a bust of me in khaki outfit for the academy and also for a private exhibition of her own works, which includes the Prince of Wales, and the Little Queen of Holland.

Hays Hammond has invited me down to South Africa again, with a promise of making my fortune, but I am not going as it takes too long.   Dick..

LEONAUR

ALSO FROM LEONAUR
AVAILABLE IN SOFTCOVER OR HARDCOVER WITH DUST JACKET

OFFICERS & GENTLEMEN *by Peter Hawker & William Graham*—Two Accounts of British Officers During the Peninsula War: Officer of Light Dragoons by Peter Hawker & Campaign in Portugal and Spain by William Graham .

THE WALCHEREN EXPEDITION *by Anonymous*—The Experiences of a British Officer of the 81st Regt. During the Campaign in the Low Countries of 1809.

LADIES OF WATERLOO *by Charlotte A. Eaton, Magdalene de Lancey & Juana Smith*—The Experiences of Three Women During the Campaign of 1815: Waterloo Days by Charlotte A. Eaton, A Week at Waterloo by Magdalene de Lancey & Juana's Story by Juana Smith.

JOURNAL OF AN OFFICER IN THE KING'S GERMAN LEGION *by John Frederick Hering*—Recollections of Campaigning During the Napoleonic Wars.

JOURNAL OF AN ARMY SURGEON IN THE PENINSULAR WAR *by Charles Boutflower*—The Recollections of a British Army Medical Man on Campaign During the Napoleonic Wars.

ON CAMPAIGN WITH MOORE AND WELLINGTON *by Anthony Hamilton*—The Experiences of a Soldier of the 43rd Regiment During the Peninsular War.

THE ROAD TO AUSTERLITZ *by R. G. Burton*—Napoleon's Campaign of 1805.

SOLDIERS OF NAPOLEON *by A. J. Doisy De Villargennes & Arthur Chuquet*—The Experiences of the Men of the French First Empire: Under the Eagles by A. J. Doisy De Villargennes & Voices of 1812 by Arthur Chuquet .

INVASION OF FRANCE, 1814 *by F. W. O. Maycock*—The Final Battles of the Napoleonic First Empire.

LEIPZIG—A CONFLICT OF TITANS *by Frederic Shoberl*—A Personal Experience of the 'Battle of the Nations' During the Napoleonic Wars, October 14th-19th, 1813.

SLASHERS *by Charles Cadell*—The Campaigns of the 28th Regiment of Foot During the Napoleonic Wars by a Serving Officer.

BATTLE IMPERIAL *by Charles William Vane*—The Campaigns in Germany & France for the Defeat of Napoleon 1813-1814.

SWIFT & BOLD *by Gibbes Rigaud*—The 60th Rifles During the Peninsula War.

LEONAUR

ALSO FROM LEONAUR
AVAILABLE IN SOFTCOVER OR HARDCOVER WITH DUST JACKET

WINGED WARFARE by William A. Bishop—The Experiences of a Canadian 'Ace' of the R.F.C. During the First World War.

THE STORY OF THE LAFAYETTE ESCADRILLE by George Thenault—A famous fighter squadron in the First World War by its commander..

R.F.C.H.Q. by Maurice Baring—The command & organisation of the British Air Force during the First World War in Europe.

SIXTY SQUADRON R.A.F. by A. J. L. Scott—On the Western Front During the First World War.

THE STRUGGLE IN THE AIR by Charles C. Turner—The Air War Over Europe During the First World War.

WITH THE FLYING SQUADRON by H. Rosher—Letters of a Pilot of the Royal Naval Air Service During the First World War.

OVER THE WEST FRONT by "Spin" & "Contact" —Two Accounts of British Pilots During the First World War in Europe, Short Flights With the Cloud Cavalry by "Spin" and Cavalry of the Clouds by "Contact".

SKYFIGHTERS OF FRANCE by Henry Farré—An account of the French War in the Air during the First World War.

THE HIGH ACES by Laurence la Tourette Driggs—French, American, British, Italian & Belgian pilots of the First World War 1914-18.

PLANE TALES OF THE SKIES by Wilfred Theodore Blake—The experiences of pilots over the Western Front during the Great War.

IN THE CLOUDS ABOVE BAGHDAD by J. E. Tennant—Recollections of the R. F. C. in Mesopotamia during the First World War against the Turks.

THE SPIDER WEB by P. I. X. (Theodore Douglas Hallam)—Royal Navy Air Service Flying Boat Operations During the First World War by a Flight Commander

EAGLES OVER THE TRENCHES by James R. McConnell & William B. Perry—Two First Hand Accounts of the American Escadrille at War in the Air During World War 1-Flying For France: With the American Escadrille at Verdun and Our Pilots in the Air

KNIGHTS OF THE AIR by Bennett A. Molter—An American Pilot's View of the Aerial War of the French Squadrons During the First World War.

LEONAUR

ALSO FROM LEONAUR
AVAILABLE IN SOFTCOVER OR HARDCOVER WITH DUST JACKET

ESCAPE FROM THE FRENCH *by Edward Boys*—A Young Royal Navy Midshipman's Adventures During the Napoleonic War.

THE VOYAGE OF H.M.S. PANDORA *by Edward Edwards R. N. & George Hamilton, edited by Basil Thomson*—In Pursuit of the Mutineers of the Bounty in the South Seas—1790-1791.

MEDUSA *by J. B. Henry Savigny and Alexander Correard and Charlotte-Adélaïde Dard* —Narrative of a Voyage to Senegal in 1816 & The Sufferings of the Picard Family After the Shipwreck of the Medusa.

THE SEA WAR OF 1812 VOLUME 1 *by A. T. Mahan*—A History of the Maritime Conflict.

THE SEA WAR OF 1812 VOLUME 2 *by A. T. Mahan*—A History of the Maritime Conflict.

WETHERELL OF H. M. S. HUSSAR *by John Wetherell*—The Recollections of an Ordinary Seaman of the Royal Navy During the Napoleonic Wars.

THE NAVAL BRIGADE IN NATAL *by C. R. N. Burne*—With the Guns of H. M. S. Terrible & H. M. S. Tartar during the Boer War 1899-1900.

THE VOYAGE OF H. M. S. BOUNTY *by William Bligh*—The True Story of an 18th Century Voyage of Exploration and Mutiny.

SHIPWRECK! *by William Gilly*—The Royal Navy's Disasters at Sea 1793-1849.

KING'S CUTTERS AND SMUGGLERS: 1700-1855 *by E. Keble Chatterton*—A unique period of maritime history-from the beginning of the eighteenth to the middle of the nineteenth century when British seamen risked all to smuggle valuable goods from wool to tea and spirits from and to the Continent.

CONFEDERATE BLOCKADE RUNNER *by John Wilkinson*—The Personal Recollections of an Officer of the Confederate Navy.

NAVAL BATTLES OF THE NAPOLEONIC WARS *by W. H. Fitchett*—Cape St. Vincent, the Nile, Cadiz, Copenhagen, Trafalgar & Others.

PRISONERS OF THE RED DESERT *by R. S. Gwatkin-Williams*—The Adventures of the Crew of the Tara During the First World War.

U-BOAT WAR 1914-1918 *by James B. Connolly/Karl von Schenk*—Two Contrasting Accounts from Both Sides of the Conflict at Sea During the Great War.

www.ingramcontent.com/pod-product-compliance
Lightning Source LLC
Chambersburg PA
CBHW021112090426
42738CB00006B/613